# *Changed Days*

## Memories of an Edinburgh Community

ALAN SPENCE

ACT ONE: 1929 to 1939
(Interval for the Second World War)
ACT TWO: 1945 and on



Hodder & Stoughton
LONDON SYDNEY AUCKLAND TORONTO

Commissioned by WINGED HORSE TOURING PRODUCTIONS, 6 The Old Schoolhouse, 1 Dean Path, Edinburgh EH4 3BG.

British Library Cataloguing-in-Publication Data
Spence, Alan
Changed days.
I. Title
822

ISBN 0-340-55853-9

First published 1991



Typeset by Keyset Composition, Colchester.
Printed in Great Britain for the educational publishing division of Hodder & Stoughton Ltd, Mill Road, Dunton Green, Sevenoaks, Kent by Clays Ltd, St Ives plc.

Cover illustration by Gainford Design Associates from an idea by the Royal Lyceum Theatre.

# Acknowledgements

THANKS FOR THE MEMORIES . . . of many Edinburgh residents – including: Josie Auld, Colin Bartie, Ian Beveridge, Mrs Brady, Mrs Adel Brownhill, Alice Capavani, Mrs Elizabeth Fernie, Norman Forsyth, Bob Gillan, Jim Grahame, Noel 'Dickie' Hamilton, Mrs Maria Hughes, Peggy Jamieson, Elsie McLean, Mr Pennycook, Jeannie Rocks, Mr Patrick Rogan, Hannah Sibson, Diana Sinclair, Billy Troup, Dr D A Walker, Mrs Watt, Harry Wright, Rev. Dr R Selby Wright, Harry Young and members of both of the People's Story reminiscence groups and the Old Town Reminiscence Group.

Acknowledgements also for help in the preparation of this play to: Liz Beevers, Bob Bertram, Mrs Elizabeth Casciani, Helen Clark, Stewart Conn, Edinburgh District Council's Museums and Art Galleries section, Hazel Enwood, Elaine Finnie, Mr Harry Hawthorne, Hamish Henderson, Betty Hepburn, Kevin Hutchins, Gwen McIlroy, Maggie MacKay, Susan Moffat, the Old Town Oral History Project, *The Pilton Story* at Craigroyston Community High School, Stewart Skirving, Bet Stivens, Terry Telford, Wester Hailes Writers Co-op and Edna Wood.

*Changed Days* was inspired by, and heralded the opening of, Edinburgh's People's Story Museum. The play was premiered by Winged Horse Touring Productions on 1st November 1988 at Muirhouse Parish Church Hall, Edinburgh.

THE CAST: Lewis Howden
Isabella Jarrett
Faye Milligan
Tracey Spence
Garry Stewart

Direction and Lighting Design by John Carnegie

*Changed Days* is derived from oral history material – the recorded memories of local people who lived through the events portrayed. The emphasis is on everyday experience although – from time to time – outside events impinge. Although the structure and texture of the play and the selection of areas of interest are not arbitrary, the play tries to reflect the (often contradictory) experiences and opinions of those portrayed.

The preparation of this show has involved many hours of poring over transcripts of existing interviews – as well as carrying out original research and interviews. Although this process has been time-consuming, it has been continually exhilarating since what the play celebrates is the resilience of community life and, in particular, the richness and vitality of its language.

The basic premiss of the play is one of a series of related and developing stories being told by a group of actors to an audience. In the original production the cast of five played many parts with usually only minimal changes of costume. Often, due to the nature of the play, they did not play closely defined characters. This published version of the script is close to the one originally performed by the Winged Horse company in 1988. For the play's revival by the Royal Lyceum in 1991 a few changes were incorporated but the text remains substantially the same.

SPECIAL THANKS to Edinburgh District Council's **People's Story Museum** and **Huntley House Museum** for all their help and for kind permission to use the photographs included in this book. Thanks also to *The Scotsman* for permission to use the photograph of 'Rubber Mill Workers' that appears opposite page 88.

# ACT ONE

(FIVE ACTORS *appear on the stage*)

1ST ACTOR Ladies and gentlemen, welcome to our historical pageant! See history in the making! Come with us down the royal mile of memory, up the high street of reminiscence. Dawdle along the esplanade of recollection and roon the back tae the stairheid of nostalgia. . . .

1ST ACTRESS All right, all right! Come on, get on with it!

1ST ACTOR Yes, yes. Now, where was I?

2ND ACTRESS History.

1ST ACTOR Of course. What year is it?

2ND ACTOR 1929.

3RD ACTRESS A momentous year. British troops evacuate the Rhineland. The R101 airship is launched.

2ND ACTRESS In the General Election, women vote for the first time. The Flapper Election!

3RD ACTRESS Labour are elected. Miss Margaret Bondfield is the first woman ever appointed to Cabinet office.

1ST ACTOR And here in Edinburgh we celebrate the sex-centenary . . .

2ND ACTRESS Hey come on, this is a family show . . .

1ST ACTOR The six hundredth anniversary (!) of the granting of a charter to the city of Edinburgh by Robert the Bruce. And here at the Usher Hall (*gestures expansively*) before an audience of 3000 people . . . (*looks at audience*) Well! Use your imagination! Here at the Usher Hall we present The Masque Of Edinburgh!

2ND ACTOR Tickets 5/—, 2/6 and 1/—, from Mr Sterling Craig at Poole's Synod Hall

1ST ACTOR Ladies and gentlemen, welcome to our historical pageant!

(*Fanfare.* TWO OF THE ACTRESSES *become an audience commenting on the pageant being presented by the others.*)

1ST ACTRESS Scene One!

3RD ACTRESS Saint Margaret achieves Christian Unity in 1087.

1ST ACTRESS Eh?

3RD ACTRESS Saint Margaret . . .

1ST ACTRESS Christian Unity?

3RD ACTRESS That's what it says here. Margaret appeals to the Culdee priests. Scotland becomes Roman Catholic.

1ST ACTRESS Eh?

3RD ACTRESS Roman Catholic.

1ST ACTRESS Try telling them that down Blackfriars Street!

3RD ACTRESS Never mind about Blackie. We're talking about history.

1ST ACTRESS But . . .

3RD ACTRESS History!

1ST ACTRESS Aye, OK.

3RD ACTRESS Scene One continues. The poor beg for alms.

1ST ACTRESS That's history all right!

3RD ACTRESS A soldier rushes in, panting and exhausted . . . (*Nobody moves so she repeats loudly.*) A soldier rushes in, panting and exhausted.

2ND ACTOR The English! The English! They have seized Carlisle and are marching north, destroying, looting and pillaging.

1ST ACTRESS Some things never change, eh!

1ST ACTOR Malcolm Canmore draws his sword.

2ND ACTRESS I beg you to seek peace with the English. Come to the church and pray for peace.

'CANMORE' I will come and pray, but not for peace, for victory! (*cheer*)

3RD ACTRESS Scene Two. Bruce, Bannockburn and Edinburgh's Charter.

1ST ACTRESS Now you're talking!

3RD ACTRESS Performed by the boys of George Watson's Boys' College.

1ST ACTRESS Oh.

3RD ACTRESS Fear not! The boys are dignified and speak in manly chord with clear enunciation.

1ST ACTRESS Thank God for that!

3RD ACTRESS Bruce addresses his army on the eve of Bannockburn. Words of wisdom and valour.

'BRUCE' Hasten to your gory bed, or to victory!

3RD ACTRESS 'Scots wha hae' is faintly heard on the organ. (*tape music*) The music swells till the hall rings with the echoes of the Scottish National Anthem!

1ST ACTRESS Yes! (*music cuts*)

3RD ACTRESS A minute later the rising curtain shows the Bruce of a later day, nearing his deathbed, as he grants the charter to the City of Edinburgh . . . (*cheers*)

1ST ACTRESS He died a few days after that, you know. Leprosy. (*They leap back, recoiling.*)

1ST ACTRESS Not too many people know that. Anyway . . .

3RD ACTRESS On with the show.

Scene Three. The Blue Blanket.

1ST ACTRESS The King presents his famous blue banner to the tradesmen of Edinburgh for rescuing him from prison.

1ST ACTRESS Prison? The King?

3RD ACTRESS The scene introduces a dainty dance.

1ST ACTRESS Reels and Pavanes.

3RD ACTRESS The Scots and the English.

1ST ACTOR Our thanks to the ladies of the Edinburgh Women Citizens' Association for the production of this scene.

3RD ACTRESS Scene Four. Flodden.

1ST ACTRESS I don't want to look.

3RD ACTRESS Flowers o the forest.

1ST ACTRESS Same old story.

3RD ACTRESS Glorious defeat.

1ST ACTRESS Let's move on.

3RD ACTRESS Scene Five.

1ST ACTOR A pretty little scene produced by Lady Margaret Sackville and friends.

1ST ACTRESS Oh aye.

3RD ACTRESS Mary Queen of Scots receives John Knox.

1ST ACTRESS More Christian Unity?

3RD ACTRESS Not quite.

1ST ACTRESS Pity. Anyway, what comes next?

3RD ACTRESS This should be right up your street.

1ST ACTRESS My street?

3RD ACTRESS Life in the Canongate.

1ST ACTRESS Great!

1ST ACTOR Originally it was a separate Burgh, you know.

1ST ACTRESS Aye, I know.

1ST ACTOR Occupied by the aristocracy and their servants. They started to move south after the Act of Union in 1707.

1ST ACTRESS Parcel of rogues!

1ST ACTOR Then we had the influx of. . . other classes. Here we have a typical tenement, what you call a Land. (*indicates rest of cast at different heights*)

2ND ACTRESS On the first floor, Lord MacSnotter, still occupying his town house.

2ND ACTOR On the ground floor, the eminent surgeon Doctor Hackit.

2ND ACTRESS Two up, a tradesman and his family.

2ND ACTOR And, right up in the attic, some labourer and his brood.

1ST ACTOR (*hanky to nose*) We won't even look in the cellar. God knows what we'll find down there.

2ND ACTRESS No, of course, we don't want to offend your sensibilities.

1ST ACTOR Obviously those who could afford it moved out of the Old Town to more . . . spacious accommodation. Come the Industrial Revolution, the place was an absolute slum.

1ST ACTRESS Quite.

3RD ACTRESS Scene Seven, Burns and Scott.

1ST ACTRESS A street scene.

3RD ACTRESS An historic meeting. Burns and the boy Scott, and old Edinburgh worthies.

1ST ACTRESS Such as?

3RD ACTRESS Sweetie Susy. Saut Maggie. Mrs Mucklemak. And a street singer.

1ST ACTRESS Now that's more like the thing.

2ND ACTRESS (*sings*)
The Bonny Wells o Wearie
The Bonny Wells o Wearie
Come let us spend a summer's day
Beside the Wells o Wearie.

3RD ACTRESS The closing of the street scene is very amusing.

2ND ACTRESS Gardyloo! (*All duck their heads.*)

1ST ACTRESS Very amusing!

3RD ACTRESS (*ignores her*) Before we leave this Masque and move on . . .

1ST ACTRESS Oh, we're moving on, are we?

3RD ACTRESS A word about the audience. (*reads*) When the audience was not clapping the choirs into extinction, it was either talking or coughing or banging the seats up and down. As audiences go, it was not perfect. (*to audience*) So, none of that from you lot!

1ST ACTRESS Listen, what year is this again?

3RD ACTRESS 1929.

1ST ACTRESS Well, how about what's happening now?

1ST ACTOR On the same day as the Masque, the Duke and Duchess of York visit Edinburgh, to unveil statues of Wallace and Bruce at the Castle.

1ST ACTRESS Aye, but . . .

1ST ACTOR The Duke inspects a guard of the Cameron Highlanders; the Duchess wears a coat of pink crepe-de-chine, with hat to match.

1ST ACTRESS Didnae even wear their crowns!

1ST ACTOR The Duke makes a stirring speech.

'DUKE OF YORK' I like to think that William Wallace and Robert the Bruce are looking down on us with pride and gratitude. For the name of Scotland today means the name of freedom, and on the foundations they laid has been reared a nation second to none.
(*Applause. Cut abruptly.*)

1ST ACTRESS This is all very fine, but it's just like the other stuff. Pageantry. Pomp. But what about real history?

2ND ACTOR Sorry?

1ST ACTRESS The people. The folk. What was really happening in 1929?

2ND ACTOR (*sings*) In 1929 it was a very good year . . .

2ND ACTRESS Was it?

1ST ACTOR It wasnae all happy days right enough.

3RD ACTRESS In fact, I'd say it was pretty grim.

2ND ACTOR My mother had about eighteen children. Nine of us survived. What with the diphtheria and the TB and the scarlet fever. That was all the rage for a while! They used to die ten a penny when that came round. Died of all sorts of troubles really. Bum troubles, infections. Or just straightforward malnutrition. They died like flies. Especially in the Canongate part, where folk were poor.

1ST ACTOR When the Duchess was here.

1ST ACTRESS Without her crown.

3RD ACTRESS In her pink crepe-de-chine.

1ST ACTOR She was being shown down the Royal Mile.

2ND ACTOR Scotland's brave highway. (*sings*)
If ae decreed that I should walk
But just one mile each day . . .

1ST ACTOR Aye. Anyway, as I was saying!

2ND ACTRESS When the Duchess was here.

3RD ACTRESS Being shown down the Royal Mile.

1ST ACTOR She stopped. Just across from John Knox's house, at Tweeddale Close. She's standing there wi her ladies-in-waiting and all her flunkeys and half a dozen toon cooncillors. And she says 'I want to see what's down there'. And all the attendants and that blocked her way and said, 'Oh no!' and they wouldnae let her pass. Then she got her eye on the next close – the World's End, and she walked across, and they're saying 'No, no, no . . .' And she's saying 'Yes, yes, yes!' And she walks right between them and marches right down the close. And the cooncillors are looking and saying 'Oh my God!' And what she must have seen! The drains and the shit and God knows what else! And she just walked in, and she looked, and she walked out again. Never said a word.

2ND ACTOR (*sings*)
O let me walk the Royal Mile
That's Scotland's brave highway . . .

2ND ACTRESS The whole place was teeming. Teeming wi life.

1ST ACTRESS Aye, the hooses were awfy buggy!

2ND ACTRESS Bugs. Beetles. Silverfish.

3RD ACTRESS And damp. Hotching wi lice. Rats.

1ST ACTRESS When the basement got flooded the rats had a swimming gala!

3RD ACTRESS You'd see the rats coming out the brewery, and they'd been eating the brewers' yeast and it made them drunk. Drunk rats, staggering all over the place!

2ND ACTRESS Teeming wi life.

2ND ACTOR We might have been ragged, but we didn't go hungry.

1ST ACTRESS You were lucky.

2ND ACTOR There was a warmth about the place. Folk looked out for one another. They were sociable.

1ST ACTRESS Never a house you couldnae go into. And none of this locking your door.

1ST ACTOR My father used to say our kitchen was like an Irishman's parlour. Everybody talking and nobody listening!

3RD ACTRESS No Irish jokes please!

1ST ACTOR Scotch Irish Day.

2ND ACTOR A special occasion for aggression!

ALL (*singing*)
Hello! Hello! We are the Blackie boys!
Hello! Hello! You'll know us by our noise!
(*The cast are swinging bits of string with a rolled up ball of paper on the end.*)

1ST ACTOR Are you Scotch or Irish?

1ST ACTRESS Scotch.

1ST ACTOR (*hits her with the ball*) Wallop!

2ND ACTOR Scotch or Irish?

2ND ACTRESS Eh . . . Irish.

2ND ACTOR (*hits her with ball*) Wallop!

3RD ACTRESS Hey you! Are you Scotch or Irish?

1ST ACTOR I'm Italian!

3RD ACTRESS Think you're smart do you! (*hits him with ball*) Wallop!

1ST ACTRESS Hey! Scotch or Irish?

2ND ACTOR Actually I'm Jewish.

1ST ACTOR Scotch Jewish or Irish Jewish?

2ND ACTOR Well . . .

1ST ACTOR, 1ST & 3RD ACTRESSES (*hit him*) Wallop!

2ND ACTRESS Ach it was all harmless fun.

2ND ACTOR Harmless!

2ND ACTRESS Come on! A rolled-up bit of paper!

3RD ACTRESS Sometimes it had a tattie inside it. Or a stone. Not so funny then.

1ST ACTRESS Oh the tensions were there all right. But I still maintain it wasnae such a bad place to live. It was neighbourly.

3RD ACTRESS Say you wanted to go to the wash house but you've got kids, somebody would say, 'Away you go, I'll watch the kids for you.' Or say you've hung your washing out, and you're away to the shops, and a big shower comes on, there was always some good samaritan would take your washing in for you.

1ST ACTRESS Or if anybody was ill, they wouldnae just lie there on their own. Somebody would come in wi a bowl of soup.

2ND ACTRESS There was always a pot of soup on the go in our house.

1ST ACTOR Hunger's good kitchen!

2ND ACTRESS Big pot of soup, simmering away.

(*The cast have now assumed definite characters, the members of a family.*)

DAUGHTER Sheep's heid broth!

MOTHER You had to steep the heid overnight in a basin. And you roasted it on the fire to get rid of the skin and the hair, and oh what a smell! Mind you, the place was gey smelly anyway, but that was something special!

DAUGHTER On a Sunday we'd have rabbit stew. That was nice and cheap. And my father liked his tripe. I couldnae even look at it!

FATHER Couldnae stomach it!

MOTHER That's right. We'd get stuff like that down the Cowgate, from what you'd call an offal butcher's.

FATHER Aye, right enough. There was quite a few awful butchers.

MOTHER Right! Come in you lot. Your tea's ready.

DAUGHTER Great!

MOTHER Not you. You'll have to wait for the second sitting.

DAUGHTER Och, I've always got to wait!

MOTHER Your faither and your brothers have been slaving away all day. They're starving.

DAUGHTER So am I.

MOTHER Well, next time you're eating your piece, maybe you'll think twice about chucking your crust on the fire.

SON Feeding the devil!

MOTHER Now, away you go or you'll get the back of my hand!

DAUGHTER But . . .

MOTHER Out!

(*A* GUIDE *interprets the scene.*)

GUIDE Ladies and gentlemen, we continue our historical pageant with this charming little tableau entitled 'Two Sittings For Dinner'. Observe, if you will, the accurately recreated interior . . .

FATHER No expense spared!

GUIDE Through there is the Room, and in here is the Kitchen.

DAUGHTER No bathroom. No even an inside toilet. The lavvy's outside on the landing, shared wi three other families on the stair. If you can stand the smell, it's one of the few places you can get a minute's peace! Can sit and read my comic. But not at night when it's dark. I hate using it then. There's no light comes in at all. What I do is leave the door just open so you get a wee bit light coming in from the stairhead. But you've got to bang the door shut if you hear somebody else coming. Whistle loud or sing at the top of your voice to let them know you're in there!

MOTHER Where is that lassie? She's under your feet till you're looking for her, then you canny see hide or hair of her.

GUIDE To continue . . . The Room is where most of the children sleep, three or four to a bed. The bed here is just a slatted wooden frame with a flock mattress on top.

FATHER Shapeless bloody thing. Lumpy. You wake up in the morning and it's moved round and pushed the slats apart and you're down between them, halfway through the bed. My back's killing me.

GUIDE Through here, just between the Room and the Kitchen, is the Lobby.

SON Tiny wee space really. Just big enough for a press wi a coal bunker in it.

GUIDE So you don't actually keep coal in the bath?

SON What bath?

MOTHER Actually we do have a bath. Big zinc thing. Hangs up behind the door in the press. Gets dragged out on a Friday night.

GUIDE So everybody has a bath once a week. Whether they need it or not! That's through here in the Kitchen of course, in front of the big blackleaded range.

SON (*sings*) Home, home on the range!

GUIDE The Kitchen, of course, is where the parents and the younger kids sleep. There's a bed recess over there, another wee bed in the corner and a bed settee against the wall. No room for much else in the way of furniture. A table. A few odd chairs. A sideboard.

MOTHER No room to swing a cat.

SON Why would you want to?

GUIDE So the Kitchen functions as a living room . . .

FATHER Sitting room . . .

SON Dining room . . .

MOTHER Bedroom . . .

FATHER Bathroom . . .

BROTHER Laundry . . .

MOTHER As well as being a kitchen.

GUIDE Right, so we've got the picture. Let's get on with the tableau. Two sittings for dinner!

(*General rammy round the table, jostling, elbowing for space.*)

MOTHER Where is that lassie?

DAUGHTER Coming!

MOTHER Here, help me dish up the soup. And, before ye ask, it's not sheep's heid broth.

DAUGHTER I know that!

SON Can tell by the smell!

DAUGHTER That stuff would make ye boke.

MOTHER Aye, well, this is made wi a nice ham bone. Got it in Campbell's.

SON What else are we getting?

MOTHER Stovies.

SON Great!

MOTHER And bread-and-butter pudding.

FATHER Talk about filling! Nothing to beat a good tightener. All I need now is a glass of soor dook to wash it down.

DAUGHTER That's something else my father liked was his soor dook. A cart would come round on a Sunday morning and you'd go down wi your jug and get it filled for a penny. A pennyworth o soor dook. And he'd drink the lot himself. None of the rest of us would touch it!

VOICE (*off stage – street cry*) Soor dook! Soor dook! Come and get your soor dook!

DAUGHTER Come on!

SON I thought you didn't like the stuff.

DAUGHTER Aye, but I like going down the High Street, seeing all the characters.

SON The buckie wives.

BUCKIE WIFE (*entering, with her creel*) Buckies! Fine buckies! Get yer fresh buckies here!

FATHER (*sings*)

When I was a laddie in Auld Reekie toon
I looked for the buckie wife comin aroon.
Wi a creel on her back, and a strap tae her broo
In each hand a tin pitcher o mussels quite fu,

ALL (*sing*)

Fine buckies, fine buckies
Noo that was her cry
Fresh mussels the day O
Please come an buy!

SON There's Balloon Bobby.

FATHER (*imitating* BOBBY) Away and get a bundle o rags son and I'll gie ye a balloon. Any auld rags missis?

MOTHER Aye, and I'm wearing them!

SON There's Spoon Willie.

DAUGHTER Hop Step and Birl.

SON Poor soul, he's no right in the heid.

DAUGHTER And neither is thon one.

SON Burn-the-bible.

DAUGHTER Or Choke-the-chicken.

SON Or Daft Sandy that marches in front o all the funerals.

DAUGHTER Four feet nothing, wi a big lum hat on his heid.

SON But he's harmless. Nobody bothers.

DAUGHTER It's that sort of place.

SON Come on and I'll show you the skeechan shop.

DAUGHTER What's that?

SON Where they sell the skeechan shandy. Open on a Sunday morning. Surefire cure for a hangover.

DAUGHTER (*peering*) God, what a pit! Cannae see a thing for smoke.

SON All the men smoking their fags and their pipes.

DAUGHTER Auld Reekie right enough!

SON Reekin and skeechan!

BUCKIE WIFE Buckies! Fresh buckies! (*to* DAUGHTER) Here, mind my pitch a minute. I'm just going in for a wee refreshment.

ALL (*sing*)

Fine buckies, fine buckies
Noo that was her cry
Fresh mussels the day O
Please come an buy.

2ND ACTOR Characters, eh! Where's yer Walter Scott noo?

3RD ACTRESS The thing is . . .

2ND ACTOR What?

3RD ACTRESS Don't you think we're getting a wee bit rose-tinted again?

2ND ACTOR I suppose when you're a child you don't know things are difficult. You would think it was great. Everything is great! What's difficult? You're getting fed, and you're amongst your own kith and kin. There's nothing difficult. Well, as a kid you don't see it.

(*Kids' games start going on round about.*)

ALL (*sing*)
In and out the dusty bluebells
In and out the dusty bluebells
In and out the dusty bluebells
I am your partner . . .

GIRLS (*sing*)
The wind the wind the wind blows high
The snow comes falling from the sky
She is handsome she is pretty
She is the girl of the golden city
Maggie and Mary and Jeannie and Betty
Shall die in the wind of the golden city . . .

2ND ACTOR Die in the wind of the golden city.

2ND ACTRESS Scotland's brave highway.

2ND ACTOR Eighteen of a family. Maybe nine survived.

1ST ACTOR Every night you'd check the list in the Evening News.

MOTHER Just a wee square with numbers on it. When your child went into the hospital, you got a number, and you looked it up in the paper. And beside your number it would have 'Gravely ill' or 'Seriously ill' or 'Making satisfactory progress.' My wee lassie went in with diphtheria. It was an isolation hospital. We were never allowed to visit. Just had to look it up in the News. Number 427. Gravely ill. Then she died.

GIRL (*sings*)
She is handsome she is pretty
She is the girl of the golden city

DAUGHTER I nearly died myself wi the measles, when I was eight. Woke up in the middle of the night, burning hot, screaming my head off. 'I don't want to die! I don't want to die!' Hanging onto my mother for dear life! And of course we couldnae afford to send for the doctor. Just had to get on with it. You survived or you didn't. And that was that.

1ST ACTOR And then there was the home-made remedies.

2ND ACTRESS Kill or cure!

MOTHER Right you! Just lie at peace and get this down you.

DAUGHTER What is it?

MOTHER Never you mind. It's good for you.

DAUGHTER (*holds nose, swallows*) Gruuch! What in God's name was that?

FATHER Right. Slap this iodine on her chest.

MOTHER OK. On wi the vinegar and brown paper.

FATHER Have ye got that auld sock? Right, fill it up wi heated salt and tie it round her throat.

DAUGHTER Phoh!

FATHER Right, pass the Ecky-pecky-anny wine! (*Takes bottle, swigs it himself.*)

MOTHER Hey!

SON Is that a poisoned thumb you've got?

DAUGHTER Aye. Beelin.

FATHER A soap and sugar poultice. That's the thing.

MOTHER And did you say you had a toothache?

DAUGHTER That's right.

MOTHER So, bite on this clove.

DAUGHTER (*moans*)

MOTHER Feeling better?

DAUGHTER (*moans, shakes head*)

FATHER We've got Gregory's Mixture, Sloan's Liniment, liquid paraffin. Here, try this.

DAUGHTER Smells horrible!

FATHER Open wide! (*holds patient's nose, forces spoonful down throat*)

DAUGHTER Grrorgh!

FATHER Just a wee bit of this and a wee bit of that.

SON Old wives' cures.

MOTHER Works wonders.

FATHER Miraculous.

SON (*sings*) It's yer Auntie Maggie's home made remedies . . .

DAUGHTER (*offstage*) Bring on the National Health!

FATHER It's coming. It's coming. Remember, it's still only 1929.
(*sings*) In 1929, it was a very good year . . .

SON Can I go out and play?

FATHER Aye, away you go.

SON Can I put on my new boots?

FATHER Makes a change fae goin barefoot, eh? Go on, wear them.

SON (*looking down at boots*) Magic, aren't they! You can run and slide on them. You can kick sparks off the tackets! (*demonstrates*)

VOICES (*offstage, calling out, mocking*) Polis boots! Polis boots! Polis boots! Polis boots!

FATHER You got them from the parish, you see. And the police distributed them. That's why they called them polis boots. And do you know what they did? They punched these holes in them so you couldnae pawn them! A wee pattern of five holes.

SON Just here. (*indicates*) One-two-three-four-five. (*counts on fingers*) Do-not-pawn-these-boots. That's what it means! Do not pawn these boots.

FATHER They didnae last long mind you. You'd kick the toes out them playin football or kick-the-can, or climbin dykes. They'd end up wi the sole flappin off them and that was them finished. Kaput! Then you were back to bare feet.

(*sings*)

In 1929, it was a very good year . . .

1ST ACTOR Suppose it was, for some.

(2ND ACTOR *becomes* WILLIAM Y DARLING – *a business man with top hat and cane.*)

3RD ACTRESS In the capital and throughout Scotland Messrs Darling and Company hold the first place in all that appertains to elegant attire.

DARLING Original model gowns to order from ten to one hundred guineas.

2ND ACTRESS A beautiful big shop in Princes Street. Just beautiful.

3RD ACTRESS Darling started off as a packman round the doors.

2ND ACTRESS A big strapping man. Very handsome.

1ST ACTRESS Arrogant. Toffee-nosed.

2ND ACTRESS But still there was something good about him.

1ST ACTOR He paid low wages.

3RD ACTRESS They all did, didn't they.

1ST ACTOR It was hard to get a job there, especially if you came from one of the poorer parts.

2ND ACTRESS It was an honour to work for him.

3RD ACTRESS He always wore a top hat.

1ST ACTRESS A right big-heid!

1ST ACTOR He had a sense of humour, mind. He told this story about the time he went down to London as an M.P. And he said . . .

DARLING You know, here I am, near enough sixty year old, and I never realised I was so well known.

1ST ACTOR How do you mean, Willie?

DARLING Well, I gets off the train at King's Cross, and I'm walking along to Westminster. And I pass all these 'ladies' (if you know what I mean!) and they all say, 'Hello Darling!'

3RD ACTRESS I remember the Left gave out this leaflet – a big cartwheel on it with William Y Darling in the middle and all these spokes linking him to the banks, the building societies, the big businesses. A big wheel encompassing the whole system and the clique that benefited from it.

DARLING In 1929, it was a very good year . . . (*exit*)

OTHERS (*calling after him*) For some!

(*Lights dim.*)

3RD ACTRESS In 1929 the R101 flew over Edinburgh. Biggest airship in the world. I remember the size of it, the size of its shadow.

2ND ACTOR A year later it was down in flames.

3RD ACTRESS The size of it, just drifting past, dead silent. I don't know, there was something beautiful about it.

1ST ACTRESS Made you feel proud.

1ST ACTOR The same year as the Duke and Duchess unveiled the statues of Wallace and Bruce.

2ND ACTRESS 1929.

3RD ACTRESS Somehow it was all part of the same thing. The same feeling.

2ND ACTRESS A new decade coming up. Everything looking good.

1ST ACTOR The Duchess wore a coat of pink crepe-de-chine.

3RD ACTRESS The first place in all that appertains to elegant attire.

1ST ACTOR Do not pawn these boots.

3RD ACTRESS A big wheel encompassing the whole system.

2ND ACTOR In 1929 I lost my job.

3RD ACTRESS In 1929 my wee girl died in the fever hospital.

1ST ACTRESS In 1929 Wall Street went *crash*!

2ND ACTOR Down in flames.

2ND ACTRESS Of course you read about things like that in the paper, but somehow it never made much of an impression. It never hit home.

3RD ACTRESS Words like Recession and Depression didn't mean very much. Yet.

1ST ACTRESS Well, you don't see it, do you?

1ST ACTOR What's difficult?

1ST ACTRESS Everything is great!

2ND ACTRESS A ha'penny worth o tiger nuts, and a ha'penny worth o buckies, and into the pictures for a penny!

1ST ACTRESS On into the Thirties!

(*Tape – 'Nice Work If You Can Get It'. Lights up.*)

3RD ACTRESS I got a job in the lemonade factory. Dunbar's. Heavy work. A dozen and a half big glass bottles in every box, and when you finish labelling a box you carry it away yourself and fling them six or seven high. Small place it is. Mr Dunbar himself makes all the syrups. Stands there like a wizard, stirring them up! He got a gold medal for it. An award. Och, it's no such a bad place to work. 8 till 12. An hour off for your dinner, then 1 till 6. That's the working day. No morning or afternoon breaks, just straight through. It's cold mind you. Stone walls, stone floors, no heating. But you're no there for comfort. You're there to work. A big rubber apron on, and big rubber boots, or clogs. Sometimes, if it's a faulty bottle, it can burst in your hand. Explode just like that. Can give you a nasty cut. Oh, I've had a few myself. But what can you do? You stop the bleeding and get back to your work.

2ND ACTRESS I'm a machinist, making overalls. It's the big heavy industrial machines we use. And what a noise they make! I'm sure it's affecting my hearing. It's a right sweat shop really. Fifty hour week we work – five and a half days – and we started off at seven shillings a week. Penny three farthings an hour! No tea-breaks mind, and the supervisor standing over you to make sure you keep up to your target. And if they think you're no going fast enough, they turn up the gauge to make the conveyor belt go faster! Oh it's a hard life, hard work. But we have a good laugh. You just have to take these things in your stride, don't you?

1ST ACTOR I work in the rubber mill. Doing the vulcanising. Big steam vulcanising chambers, and you swing these big carriages loaded up wi coats and boots and things. And the heat's terrific. Your feet are roasting because it's all steam pipes underneath the floor. Pretty grim really. And if you're on the machine that spreads out the sheets of rubber, half the time you're doped up wi the naphtha fumes. And of course, this naphtha's got a low flash point – very inflammable. Place is a death trap if you think about it. Luckily I've only ever seen the one bad accident – fella spilled the naphtha over himself and it caught fire. Had to throw pails of water over him before they got it out. Oh aye, it's a dangerous job right enough. But it's a job.

(*Tape – 'Nice Work If You Can Get It'*)

2ND ACTOR Nice work.

1ST ACTOR We're the lucky ones.

2ND ACTRESS We've got jobs.

3RD ACTRESS Gainfully employed.

1ST ACTOR It means we can get by.

3RD ACTRESS Make ends meet.

2ND ACTRESS With a bit of help from the neighbours.

MOTHER We've got a sort of syndicate.

FATHER Sounds like something out a gangster picture. George Raft!

MOTHER Somebody gets paid on a Thursday night. They go round all the other families that are in it. Give them ten bob or a pound. The next night somebody else gets paid, and they go round and do the same. By the time everybody's got their wages, the money's been circulated right round. Works out really fine.

FATHER (GANGSTER'S *voice*) Hi, I'm from the syndicate. I've come to collect my ten bob.

SON Daftie!

MOTHER And if all else fails, there's always the pawn. The one down the World's End Close is rare and handy.

DAUGHTER Suppose I'll have to go down in the morning and get my da's suit out.

MOTHER He'll need it for the weekend.

DAUGHTER Then back in again on Monday.

FATHER Helps see us through the week. As long as you keep on top of it, don't let it get out of hand. I've seen some folk get themselves in a terrible fankle. Leave something in that long that the interest just mounts up and up. Ends up they canny pay it at all so they just let it go.

MOTHER Then there's the ones that get something to pay up, then they pawn it and sell the ticket.

FATHER That lot up the stairs did that wi a three piece suite. Carted it up all these stairs then down again the following week. Finished up wi the bailiffs coming in, threatening them wi a warrant sale. But I don't think they had anything worth selling!

MOTHER So how did they get out of that, then, without getting the jail?

FATHER God knows. Must have dreamed up something else. Robbing Peter to pay Paul. We'll probably hear them flitting sometime, in the middle of the night.

MOTHER Doing a moonlight!

SON I heard another story about them as well.

DAUGHTER Oh did you now?

SON Aye. You know the oldest son?

FATHER Big glaikit looking gommerel?

The old Canongate

Outside tap

Buckie Wife

Barrie's Trip

SON That's him. Well, it seems he was in the habit of pawning his alarm clock.

MOTHER Never had much use for it I suppose, no having any work to get up for.

FATHER Neither work nor want.

SON Anyway, he would put this clock in every Monday, get it out again on the Friday. And he'd do the same thing every week, so the pawnbroker got used to him coming in, and he'd just take the wee parcel off him and give him the money. So one Monday the boy comes in, and the man's busy and he just says 'Is it the usual?' And the boy says 'Aye.' So the man just takes it off him and puts it up beside the rest of the clocks. But then after a few days, he noticed a terrible smell, and he says to the wee laddie that's his assistant, 'What in the name of God is that?' And it was coming fae the shelf where all the clocks were sitting. And they picked up the boy's parcel, and what a smell! And they opened it up, and here, inside was a rotten sheep's heid!

DAUGHTER What a bowf!

FATHER I don't know where you get half of these stories from. Sometimes I think you make them up. (*exit*)

SON I do not!

MOTHER Here, it's time I started making the tea.

DAUGHTER As long as it's no sheep's heid broth!

MOTHER No it is not. Now you, away and get a new mantle for the gas. That one's spluttering away.

DAUGHTER Och but . . .

MOTHER No buts. Go! And don't break it this time.

DAUGHTER It's no fair. The stupid things are that delicate they crumble if you even look at them.

SON Just like you!

MOTHER They crumble if you run up the road wi them in your pocket, you mean! Or play chases wi your pals, or stop for a game of peevers!

DAUGHTER I never!

MOTHER Straight there, straight back, and careful how you carry it. Here. (*hands her the pennies*)

DAUGHTER (*sniffs*) The pennies smell of gas.

MOTHER Meter's just been emptied. That's the rebate. We're rich. Five bob extra in the kitty!

SON (*sarky*) Great!

MOTHER No, but it's our turn for the menage pay-out as well. And it's divvy-time coming up at the Co-op. So we're quids in. We're laughing.

DAUGHTER So you're splashing out on a new gas mantle!

MOTHER Cheeky monkey! Away you go before I take the back of my hand to you!

DAUGHTER I'm going! I'm going!

MOTHER And listen! Your father said he'd maybe bring home a wee surprise. If you hurry you'll be back before he gets in from his work.

DAUGHTER But I thought you didn't want me to hurry!

MOTHER You can be quick and still be careful. Now come on. Scat!

DAUGHTER (*To* SON) I wonder what his wee surprise'll be this time?

SON I wonder!

DAUGHTER Started off with his wee crystal set.

SON The cat's whiskers!

DAUGHTER Just about as footery as this bloomin gas mantle!

SON Had to use earphones to hear anything.

DAUGHTER Then it was the valves.

SON And his first loudspeaker so we could all hear at once.

DAUGHTER Half the folk in the stair crowding round for a wee listen! Crackle Crackle! Shhhhh!

SON Hey, maybe we'll get mains electricity and he'll get a proper mains set that plugs into the light.

DAUGHTER No more gas mantles? That'll be the day! (*exits*)

(*Lights change.* FATHER *enters carrying a radio.*)

FATHER It's a really good set. And I got a smashing big accumulator in Brown's. Second-hand, but it's a beauty. Shouldnae run down every five minutes like the old one! (SON *carries radio over to special table.*) We'll be able to hear the news loud and clear. (*starts tinkering*)

MOTHER Prefer a bit o music myself. Henry Hall.

SON Takes ages to warm up.

(*Freeze as* 2ND ACTRESS *speaks from the side.*)

2ND ACTRESS Five minutes later.

FATHER There!

(MOTHER *and* FATHER *start to dance to the music.*)

DAUGHTER (*Enters, carrying aloft a little box*) Made it! All the way from the shop in one piece. (*responds to music*) Hey! That's great! (*starts dancing, drops box*) Aw naw!

MOTHER I told you to be careful!

DAUGHTER It was an accident!

MOTHER Now you'll need to go and get another one. Honest to God, you must think we're made of money!

DAUGHTER But you said we were rich.

MOTHER We've got a few miserable shillings over the odds. Doesn't mean we can throw it away.

SON Maybe I should go this time. In case there's *another* accident!

(*She sticks out tongue at him. He goes. Music on radio changes to slower tempo.*)

FATHER Hey. Ye dancing?

(MOTHER *and* FATHER *start to dance.*)

DAUGHTER You did say we were rich.

MOTHER So I did, hen.

DAUGHTER See if we were really rich, would we go away for a holiday?

MOTHER Listen to Lady Muck!

FATHER We'll get away, for the odd day here and there. We can walk out to Liberton. It's nice out there.

DAUGHTER Walk?

FATHER Or take the tram to Porty.

MOTHER Or the bus out to the zoo.

FATHER D'you know what they call that bus?

DAUGHTER What?

FATHER The wee stinker. Just like you, eh!

DAUGHTER It is not!

MOTHER Anyway, you'll be getting your day out wi Baillie Barrie's Trip.

(2ND ACTRESS *enters as* DAUGHTER'S FRIEND, THERESA.)

DAUGHTER Barrie's Trip! (*to audience, visualising it*) There I'll be wi my tinny on a bit of tape, slung over my shoulder. Maybe a new pair of white rubbers.

THERESA Tanner a pair!

DAUGHTER We'll meet at the bus-stop, just at the Lyric. We'll line up in rows, and the two pipers'll start up and march us right down into Waverley Station! (*mimics piping, whines 'Scotland the Brave'*)

THERESA And Daft Sandy Scobie's up at the front wi his big lum hat, and he's singing away.

BOTH (*sing*)
O we're no awa tae bide awa,
We're no awa tae leave you.
We're no awa tae bide awa,
We'll aye come back and see you.

DAUGHTER And we're on the train . . .

THERESA And everybody's cheering and waving and singing . . .

DAUGHTER And it's out to Ratho or somewhere. Just a big field . . .

THERESA And there's all these sports, and races. Three-legged race, egg and spoon, sack race, the lot . . .

DAUGHTER If you're lucky you win a prize!

THERESA Then everybody gets a sausage roll and a bag of buns . . .

DAUGHTER And an orange or an apple, and a glass of milk . . .

THERESA Or your tinny full of tea . . .

DAUGHTER Then it's back on the train, and singing all the way hame.

BOTH (*sing*)
Old Edinburgh once more.
It's the place that I adore.
Why I hope to live and I hope to see
Old Edinburgh once more.

O we're no going to Barrie's Trips,
We're no going again,
We're no going to Barrie's Trips
Cause it always comes on rain.

THERESA But you always do go again.

DAUGHTER I know. Cause it's great! (*to* PARENTS) Hey, d'you know my wee pal Theresa got into trouble for going on Barrie's Trip?

MOTHER What for?

DAUGHTER Because she's a Catholic, and it's only supposed to be for Protestants.

MOTHER Away ye go! That's a lot of rubbish!

DAUGHTER No, it's true. She told me. She got a penance for going to Barrie's. She had to kneel in front of the Sacred Heart for ages and ages.

FATHER Damn shame.

DAUGHTER She said it was worth it.

THERESA I just thought of Margaret Sinclair and it didn't seem so bad.

MOTHER I mind o Margaret Sinclair when she was just a wee lassie. Lived in Blackfriars Street. Number 13, right at the top.

FATHER Her father was a scaffie. Swept the streets.

MOTHER She worked in McVitie's biscuit factory. Your auntie Jessie knew her well. Said she was a really lovely girl. Never said an unkind word to anybody. It was no surprise when she became a nun.

FATHER She went to London, didn't she?

MOTHER That's right. Joined a convent down there. She was only twenty-five when she died. Tragic really.

FATHER Och well, you know what they say. Only the good die young.

THERESA It was TB she had. In her throat. And she never complained once. Even though she was in terrible pain. And towards the end she was lying there gasping for breath and a wasp came and stung her right in the throat. But still she managed to smile. And all the other sisters said she looked as if she was smiling at the angels.

DAUGHTER Now there's talk about making her a saint.

MOTHER The first saint fae the factory floor!

THERESA (*sings*)
She is handsome, she is pretty
She is the girl of the golden city . . .

MOTHER They say there's been all sorts of miracles. People praying to her and being cured.

FATHER Well, I don't know about that.

MOTHER I believe it. Theresa said she prayed to her for money to go to the pictures and she found threepence.

MOTHER Sometimes I think Theresa says more than her prayers!

DAUGHTER She told me some lovely things.

THERESA (*beckons her over*) Just before my da took ill, I had the same dream twice. There was these two men in pure white suits and white bow ties. And they were sort of beckoning, like they wanted somebody to come with them. And standing right behind them was Our Lady, all shining.

DAUGHTER Aw!

THERESA And then when my da was dying, just at the end, he said 'Look at the angels!' And he pointed in front of him and said 'They're lovely. Like wee girls making their first communion!' And that was the last words he ever said.

DAUGHTER That's beautiful.

THERESA Wee girls making their first communion. I remember mine. My mother rattled up a dress for me. White voile, wi a wee lace band. And I threaded a nice white satin ribbon through it, and a nice big bow at the back. And a wee veil. And a wee crown of flowers in my hair.

DAUGHTER (*turns back to* PARENTS) You know, I think it must be all right being a Catholic. Their churches are much nicer with all the statues and everything. And you get all these wee holy pictures and things.

FATHER You better not let John Cormack hear you talking like that!

MOTHER That headcase!

FATHER They say he's quite a decent bloke.

MOTHER He's a menace. Protestant Action. I don't know!

(1ST ACTOR *enters as* CORMACK, *steps up*)

CORMACK If I were dictator of Edinburgh, Edinburgh would be one hundred percent Protestant. Protestant Dictator Cormack! What would I do? First I would call a great celebration march through the capital, hailing our faith, rallying other cities. Next I would nullify all Roman Catholic authority in schools and appoint my own teachers. I will issue orders to all Protestant churches in the city to carry out the vows they took upon ordination. I shall burn down the slums, give no compensation to their landlords. Yes, my friend, I am aware that we are talking primarily about the areas of central Leith and the Old Town, which just happen to coincide with the densest concentrations of the Roman Catholic population. Burn them out! I want Edinburgh to give the lead to this country, and to Europe, in how to deal with the Roman Catholic menace. Let us fire the latent Protestant spirit in this city. Let us make it a centre of true

Protestant culture, and Edinburgh will stir the world! No Popery! *(raises clenched fist)*

2ND ACTOR At one point this man was addressing rallies of three, four, five thousand people. He summoned up ten thousand folk to demonstrate in the High Street against a Catholic Reception at the City Chambers. He was carried shoulder-high on to North Bridge.

2ND ACTRESS Should have chucked him over it!

1ST ACTRESS He raised a crowd of 30,000 to disrupt the Eucharistic Congress.

3RD ACTRESS Can you believe this was happening? In Edinburgh! In the 1930s! Folk at each other's throats over religion!

2ND ACTOR Atomisation of the proletariat, brother. As old as the class struggle. But there were folk taking to the streets for other reasons in the Thirties. There were things worth demonstrating about.

2ND ACTRESS Look! Come and see! It's the hungry marchers!

*(The cast form up in a stylised march, carrying flags and singing 'The Internationale'.)*

ALL *(singing)*
Arise, ye starvelings, from your slumbers!
Arise, ye criminals of want!
For reason in revolt now thunders
And at last ends the age of cant.

*(They continue to hum the song under the dialogue.)*

2ND ACTRESS Four abreast we marched in columns, with bands and banners, a mobilised army in miniature – the Hunger Marchers.

3RD ACTRESS We marched for work and for bread. We marched for the 400,000 unemployed.

1ST ACTOR From all over Scotland, we were on the march.

2ND ACTRESS The Aberdeen and Dundee contingents linked up with Fife in Kirkcaldy.

3RD ACTRESS The Ayrshire contingent linked up with Lanarkshire and came in through Shotts and East Calder.

2ND ACTOR Renfrewshire and Dunbartonshire came to Glasgow, then out through Coatbridge and Airdrie, Bathgate and Broxburn.

2ND ACTRESS Along with them marched a women's section!

1ST ACTOR The Glasgow men came through Kilsyth and Falkirk. They joined forces with Stirlingshire and marched on through Bo'ness.

2ND ACTRESS We met up at Corstorphine. We were a thousand strong! The Edinburgh marchers came out to meet us, and on we went, into the city!

3RD ACTRESS 20,000 gathered to welcome us at the Mound. It was that big a crowd most folk couldn't hear the speeches! We marched on down to the Meadows at Holyrood – down the Royal Mile to the gates of the Palace.

2ND ACTOR Right through the gates and into the Palace grounds!

2ND ACTRESS Can you imagine it! The red flag paraded at the royal palace!

3RD ACTRESS Edinburgh had never seen the like!

ALL (*singing*)

Then, comrades, come rally
And the last fight let us face.
The Internationale
Unites the human race.

2ND ACTOR It looks like we'll be staying in the park the night, lads. The 'authorities' can find no accommodation for us. We can stay here or sleep in the street.

1ST ACTOR Well then, we'll sleep in the street. But by God we'll pick the street to sleep in!

3RD ACTRESS Picture it – Princes Street on a cool clear summer night. The Castle lit up by floodlights. Theatre-goers and diners strolling along, taking the evening air . . .

2ND ACTOR Right, boys, this is it. This is your bed for the night!

2ND ACTRESS We spread ourselves out, we took up the pavement and part of the roadway. The police were out in force, but they stood back and didn't interfere.

1ST ACTOR The greatest street in Europe, and look at it! Turned into a dormitory!

2ND ACTRESS The Castle lights were switched off.

1ST ACTOR (*sings*) Let's turn off the lights and go to sleep!

(*The others throw abuse in his direction.*)

3RD ACTRESS Goodnight!

2ND ACTOR Enjoy your feather bed!

(*They sleep. The lights dip to denote the passing night. With dawn,* ONE MARCHER *wakes first and plays reveille on a bugle. The others are rudely awakened!*)

1ST ACTRESS Sleep well?

3RD ACTRESS A wee bit draughty was it no?

2ND ACTOR The next night the 'authorities' managed to find accommodation for every last one of us. We had made our point!

2ND ACTRESS We had made them sit up and take notice.

2ND ACTOR The march is over, boys, but the struggle goes on. And it's going to be harder and grimmer than ever.

(*Return to 'interior'.* FATHER *is listening to radio. Rest of the family – including* YOUNGER DAUGHTER *– busy with household chores.*)

MOTHER Anything on the wireless about that march?

FATHER Nothing much. Papers played it down as well.

MOTHER Suppose it's to be expected.

FATHER Sweep it under the carpet.

MOTHER Pretend it never happened.

DAUGHTER Get back to the grind.

YOUNGER DAUGHTER Soldier on.

(MOTHER *hands* YOUNGER DAUGHTER *some coins.*)

MOTHER Here, away to Campbell's the butchers and get a shillingy fry. Oh, and take the pillowslip and get a tanner's worth of old tea-bread out the bakery.

YOUNGER DAUGHTER Big feed the night!

MOTHER Och well, it's the weekend.

YOUNGER DAUGHTER (*to audience*) It's always me that gets sent. I hate going to the butchers too. Whole sides of beef hanging up, dripping onto the sawdust, and the butcher's apron all spattered wi blood. Yuk! (*holds out money*) Shillingy fry please. It's quite good really, what you get. Bit of meat, boiling beef, sausages, a chop. And my ma'll fry it all up. Great! Now, one thing I don't mind getting is this bag of tea-bread. You get tons of it, and nobody'll ever miss a wee bit. Or two! And if I'm out doing this, somebody else'll get landed with doing the brasses and cleaning the grate. That *always* gets done on a Friday night. Down on your hands and knees, scrubbing and polishing, and blackleading the range. Murder! So maybe I'll just take my time, dawdle a wee bit! The place is just coming to life. There's Daft Sandy again, wi his lum hat. Must be looking for a funeral! Oh no! There's Catty

Annie. Do you know her? Looks like she's coming fae the mortuary, doesn't she? All dressed in black, dead sombre like. (Hey, that's quite good, isn't it? Dead sombre!) Anyway, she comes round the doors wi her big basket, asks if you've any cats you want rid of. Of course, sometimes folk are only too glad to do it. Maybe their cat's sick, needs to be put down. And she pays a shilling. No questions asked. My mother says she takes them for experimentation. The Burke and Hare of the cat world! My mother chases her if she comes to the door. She doesn't believe in it. Here, talking about my mother, I better get up the house wi her messages or I'll get hung!

MOTHER Where've you been?

YOUNGER DAUGHTER There was big queues at all the shops. (*winks at audience*)

MOTHER Aye, well. You can give your sister a hand wi the brasses.

YOUNGER DAUGHTER That's no fair!

MOTHER It is so. She's already done the range while you were out dawdling.

YOUNGER DAUGHTER Och!

MOTHER Get on wi it!

DAUGHTER Come on! You know I'm going to the dancing. And I canny get out till I've finished this.

YOUNGER DAUGHTER The dancing? It's all right for some!

DAUGHTER Oh, it's really magic so it is. The music and the coloured lights, and just, the whole *atmosphere*.

YOUNGER DAUGHTER Where'll you go?

DAUGHTER Maybe the Marine Gardens out at Porty. That's the biggest ballroom in Europe you know.

YOUNGER DAUGHTER Away!

DAUGHTER It is. I read it. Sometimes you get 2000 people there. It's a beautiful floor.

MOTHER Mind you don't miss your tram back if you go there.

DAUGHTER If I do we can walk it. There'll be a whole crowd of us. It's always a good laugh.

MOTHER Maybe some nice fella'll walk you home!

DAUGHTER Maybe! Hey, d'you know what you do if some wee creep asks you? You tell him you live in Dalkeith!

FATHER Maybe you should go somewhere in town, somewhere nearer. But not Fairlie's. I've heard about the crowd that goes there.

DAUGHTER I went there once. Never again!

SON How about McDonald's? Or Stewart's at Abbeymount?

DAUGHTER I was talking to one of the dancing partners there. She gets paid just about nothing.

MOTHER Aye, well, I don't know if I approve of this dancing partner business. Some of these girls, you know, get 'signed out.'

FATHER It's no right.

MOTHER And I've heard stories about the Kosmo.

FATHER That's one place you *won't* be going!

DAUGHTER I wouldn't go near it.

FATHER And you can stay away from that Excelsior place as well. I've heard it's a bit rough.

DAUGHTER They stamp your hand on the way in. Otherwise folk would just let their pals in by the fire exit!

MOTHER And that Maxim's place at Tollcross. What is it they call it now?

FATHER The Cavendish.

SON The manager's called The Pansy King! He was prosecuted for you-know-what!

MOTHER Ssshhhh! (*Puts finger to her lips shoshing him with a glance at the younger girl.*)

DAUGHTER Maybe we'll go to the Puggienut.

YOUNGER DAUGHTER Puggienut!

DAUGHTER You can get in on tick, tell them you'll pay next week!

MOTHER You don't want to start that. Paying things up.

DAUGHTER What about the shilling-a-week man?

MOTHER That's different. That's for necessities. Clothes for you lot.

DAUGHTER I think the dancing's a necessity!

SON (*to* MOTHER) You used to go, didn't you?

MOTHER Aye, but in those days it *was* dancing. I mean *real* dancing. The Waltz and the Quickstep and the Foxtrot. Not like this stuff they're doing now. Charleston and what have you.

DAUGHTER Black Bottom!

SON (*pretending to be in dance hall*) I was wondering if I could have the last dance.

DAUGHTER All right.

SON The thing is . . .

DAUGHTER What?

SON Well, I would offer to walk you home, but . . .

DAUGHTER But what?

SON Well I heard you telling that wee fella you live in Dalkeith. And I've got my work in the morning.

(*They all laugh.*)

MOTHER Oh well, you know what they say. Marriages are made on the dance-floor!

FATHER Or at the pictures!

YOUNGER DAUGHTER Can I get a couple of jam-jars? Charlie Chaplin's on at the Lyric!

MOTHER Last week it was Tom Mix at the Starry. You'll be wanting to go to the pictures every week now.

YOUNGER DAUGHTER I only go twice in a blue moon!

MOTHER OK, take the jam-jars.

YOUNGER DAUGHTER Thanks! (*runs off*)

MOTHER And straight home when it's finished, mind!

FATHER You're only young once, eh?

MOTHER Mind we used to sit in that flea-pit?

FATHER What a scratcher!

MOTHER You'd sit through the adverts and the news and the coming attractions and the wee picture and the big picture.

FATHER And you'd sit through the whole lot again if you didn't get put out!

MOTHER Och aye, you need your wee bit escape, don't you? You need your entertainment.

FATHER Mind you, I still think you canny beat a good old-fashioned sing-song.

(*Lights change to evening 'interior'. A* NEIGHBOUR *has come in.*)

NEIGHBOUR (*sings*)
When I grow too old to dream,
I'll have you to remember

(OTHERS *join in*)

And when I grow too old to dream
Your love will live in my heart . . .
So kiss me, my sweet
And so let us part
And when I grow too old to dream
Your love will live in my heart.

(*A moment's silence, then* SON *joins in with a music-hall song to the tune of 'D'ye ken John Peel'.*)

SON (*sings*)
Dae ye mind Lang Syne
When the family numbered nine
18 boab wis faither's wages
That included overtime.
How the mothers they did rave
And the bairns they did slave
And the work was never done
Till the morning.

Wee Jock's breeks wid need a patch
On the pairt he used to scratch.
Mother stitched on a bit flannel
Though the colours didnae match.
And he was prood as Punch
O the piece he ca'ed a lunch
As he whistled off tae school
In the morning.

Times have changed noo Jock smokes fags
And his breeks are Oxford bags.
He goes jazzin tae the Palais
In the claes he calls Glad Rags.
For he courts a lass ye see
Wi curly lashes at her ee
And it's the fashion tae come hame
In the morning.

Then there's Jessie o that ilk
Powdered face and dressed in silk.

Mighty me, ye wouldnae think
She aince carried morning milk.
She's a lady now ye know
Though she cannae darn or sew
And her mother's that tae dae
In the morning.

Ye may laugh but aye it's true
And some day my word ye'll rue
When the bairns turn up their noses
Cause it's only Sheep's Heid Stew.
As they pack up their school bags
They'll be askin ye for fags.
It's the coming generation
Some fine morning!

(*cheers, applause*)

FATHER Get out the cards. We'll have a game of rummy.

SON I've got a better idea. We'll play a game of forfeits!

DAUGHTER You're on!

NEIGHBOUR Who's going first?

SON We'll cut the cards for it.

NEIGHBOUR Right! (*cuts cards*) Five.

(*They each cut cards in turn.*)

SON Three.

FATHER Eight.

MOTHER Ten.

DAUGHTER Two! OK. What's it going to be?

(*Others go into a huddle.*)

NEIGHBOUR Right, we've decided. You've to open up the windae, and shout down into the street . . . (*whispers in ear*)

DAUGHTER Naw! I couldnae shout that!

NEIGHBOUR Oh well, that's your forfeit.

DAUGHTER All right! All right! I'll do it. (*braces herself, goes to window, shouts*) My ma had a bairn to a darkie this mornin!

(*Covers her face, turns away. General hilarity.*)

DAUGHTER (*to* SON) OK, now it's you!

SON I know!

(*huddle*)

DAUGHTER So! It's gettin quite busy out there now.

SON I noticed that, aye.

MOTHER Pubs emptying. Quite a crowd. And we were thinking they could do wi a bit of entertainment.

SON Is that right?

NEIGHBOUR So we want you to go down and give them a song.

DAUGHTER Just like these Glasgow keelies that come busking round the streets.

SON Thanks! Any special song you'd like? Any requests?

NEIGHBOUR How about 'The Spaniard that blighted my life!'

SON Sorry, I don't know all the words.

MOTHER Come on, you can sing anything. Just get on with it!

FATHER We'll both do it!

SON Aye, all right!

(*Both men exit and the women go over to the window to watch them.*)

MOTHER Watch out for the meths drinkers in the close!

NEIGHBOUR They've broken the gas mantle again, making their red biddy.

MOTHER The place is swarmin wi folk.

DAUGHTER Hey, here they come!

MEN (*singing offstage*)
I belong tae West Port
Land of Burke and Hare
And I will refuse tae flit
Heave awa, we're no deid yet!

DAUGHTER Oh God, look! It's the polis doing their rounds!

NEIGHBOUR Who is it, can you see?

DAUGHTER There's two or three of them. I can see big Death, him that's awful peely wally looking.

NEIGHBOUR He does look like Death, doesn't he? That dour-looking white face he's got.

MOTHER Death warmed up.

DAUGHTER (*shouts down*) Here's Death coming!

MOTHER Hurry up or you'll get arrested!

NEIGHBOUR It's just like when you're wee, isn't it? You don't have to be doing anything, you just take to your heels when you see them coming.

MOTHER Quite right too. Unless you wanted a thick ear!

NEIGHBOUR Is there anybody else there?

DAUGHTER Looks like Basher.

MOTHER And Gentle Annie.

NEIGHBOUR Yon big teuchter. He's anything but gentle! You know, my father once got 30 days for that big so-and-so. My da was coming down Abbeymount, and he'd had a drink in the Regent Buffet, ken. He wasnae what you call drunk, mind, he'd just had one or two. But Gentle Annie stopped him and grabbed him, and that was fatal. Cause my da was strong, you know, a big strong man, and he just got him and threw him over the dyke. Fortunately it was the low end of the dyke. If it had been the high end he'd have killed him. But that was it. He got 30 days. Drunk and disorderly. Assaulting a police officer.

MOTHER Still. It would be a helluva place without the polis.

(*Dramatic chord. Police officer appears.*)

MERRILEES I'm glad you said that, madam. My name is Merrilees. Willie Merrilees. And I'm gonnae clean up this town.

DAUGHTER Joined the cleansing department has he?

NEIGHBOUR Jumped-up wee bachle!

MOTHER D'you know he was too wee to get into the polis when he first tried. Had to get in the back door sort of thing. Got a special dispensation.

DAUGHTER Now that's no fair. He got in because he was tough. And brave. Used to work at Leith Docks, doing his security bit. And he was forever saving folk from drowning, folk that fell in the harbour and that. Saved a lot of weans that way so he did.

MOTHER Och, if you ask me, he used to chuck them in so he'd look good jumping in to rescue them!

MERRILEES I would remind you, missis, that there's such a thing as slander. Everything you say has been noted down and may be used in my autobiography.

(*He has been getting himself dressed in women's clothes.*)

Now. (*to audience*) You may be wondering why I'm dressed like this. (*to someone at back*) I heard that! (*pause*) And it's not true! I'm dressed like this because I'm on a case! Any more smart remarks and I'll nick the lot of yous. Right? (*puts on wig*) Right!

(*Exits, giving blast on police whistle.*)

NEIGHBOUR I don't know! See some of the things that go on nowadays.

DAUGHTER We don't know the half of it.

MOTHER I see that one upstairs is yon way. (*Gestures with hands, makes shape of big belly.*)

NEIGHBOUR She's no!

MOTHER She is.

NEIGHBOUR Is she gettin married then?

MOTHER She'll have to, won't she?

NEIGHBOUR Oh well. You make your bed, you lie on it. If you know what I mean!

MOTHER I was hearing about that Kosmo club, down Swinton Row.

NEIGHBOUR Swinton Row's notorious for it.

MOTHER As bad as that James's Court.

DAUGHTER Kelly's Paradise.

NEIGHBOUR Aye, I've heard about the madam there and her brood, all dressed up in feathers and furs.

DAUGHTER Kelly's Angels they call them.

MOTHER Angels!

DAUGHTER The thing is, some of them can be awful nice lassies.

NEIGHBOUR Nice?

DAUGHTER Well, you know what I mean. Here, did I ever tell you about the crowd I met in Fairlie's?

MOTHER You did not.

DAUGHTER Well, the fleet was in, so the place was jampacked. And me and my friend got in pally wi this nice set of girls. And we were that young we didnae know anything. And one of these girls says 'Come away into the cloakroom for a snifter.' And we'd had a wee bottle of Australian wine. Thought we were really fast! So we went with them, and one of them says, 'We're all on the game.' And I didnae know what they meant, and my pal whispered it to me, and I says 'Oh my God!' But what I'm saying is they were really nice, you know. Good company. And generous.

MOTHER Aye, that's the trouble. They're generous wi everything!

(*Lights down. Spot on* MERRILEES *in women's clothes, different coloured wig from before.*)

MERRILEES Pssst! It's me again. Merrilees. Different wig this time. I'm on another assignment you see. (*looks about him, furtive*) The Kosmo club. I'm sure you know the sort of place it is. A sink of iniquity. One door in and two doors out. Well, I'm going to close it down. Get rid of these vermin once and for all. These pimps that live off young girls. Not to mention the pansies – blackmailers half of them. Make you sick. And the worst of the lot is this Ashe Bernard, the scum that owns this place. You know what he does? He lures these young girls to Edinburgh by advertising for dance hostesses. Dance hostesses! Offers them ten bob a week and tuppence a dance. Sets them up in accommodation, gives them clothes and jewellery and what not, and he makes them sign for everything so they're completely dependent. Then by the time they find out they're expected to provide other services, it's too late, they're trapped. He's got a hold over them. Well, it's a hold that's just about to be broken. Just check my handbag. (*brings out baton, brandishes*) There we are. Solid that is. Made from the dock gates at Leith. (*puts it back in bag*) Right! In we go!

(*Coloured lights – 30s jazz*)

BERNARD Well, hello there, darling! Are you dancing?

MERRILEES No, it's just the way I'm standing. *(blows police whistle, whips off wig)* Right! Nobody move! This is a police raid. You're all under arrest! *(shouts off)* All right, Mr Ashe Bernard, the game's up! And you needn't try getting out the back door because I've got half a dozen good men out there. Look at him! The Vice King of Edinburgh, snivelling like a child! I do believe he's soiled his clothing! What a state to get into, eh? Assign that officer with no sense of smell to escort him to the paddy wagon! Right, now, the rest of you. Line up. 'Ladies' on one side. 'Gentlemen' on the other. 'Instructresses' over here. 'Male frequenters' down here. Now, I see from the list of those signed in this evening, we have several ministers of the Church, a Member of Parliament, a Court of Session Judge, and Sergeant William Merrilees himself! Not to mention Charlie Chaplin, Ramsay MacDonald and Mickey Mouse! *(scans list)* Prince this . . . the Duke of that . . . I see the Chief Constable's with us as well! Good evening to you sir! *(chucks away list)* All right, let's have your real names. You first. What's your name? And where do you work? Oh, you don't work? Part of the leisured classes are we? *(turning away)* Book him. In fact, book the lot of them! You're all nicked! *(exit, blowing whistle)*

*(Coloured lights down. Ordinary lighting on two women at their windows.)*

NEIGHBOUR So, they managed to close the place down.

MOTHER Raided it.

NEIGHBOUR I heard there was MPs and ministers there, among the customers.

MOTHER I heard there was royalty!

NEIGHBOUR And the Chief of Police!

MOTHER Scandalous!

NEIGHBOUR Damned disgrace.

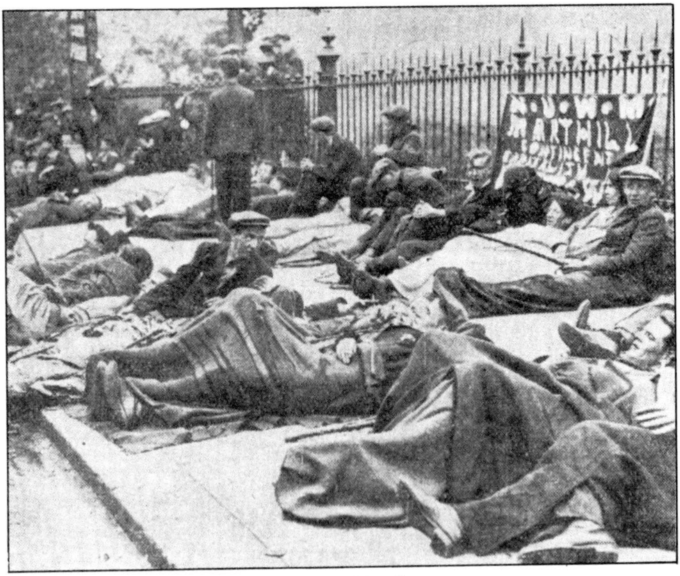

Hunger March

Bathtime . . .

Rubber Mill Worke

Wester Hailes –
the planners' dream

MOTHER Don't know what the world's coming to.

NEIGHBOUR Naw.

MOTHER Especially this place.

NEIGHBOUR Aye.

MOTHER Here, I was talking to Mrs Dolan the other day, and she said they're getting moved to a new house out in Pilton.

NEIGHBOUR That's because one of the bairns has got TB.

MOTHER That's right. They were put right to the top of the housing list. Got to go, whether they want to or not. They've got to go out the town. No option.

NEIGHBOUR Och well, the houses are nice. My sister and her family are out there. Three room and kitchen.

MOTHER You'd get lost in it!

NEIGHBOUR Aye, after what you're used to here.

MOTHER I don't know that I'd fancy it myself. Away out there, miles from anywhere, not knowing any of the folk.

NEIGHBOUR They say it's nice and fresh mind you. My sister likes it fine. Course, she's a churchgoer. Makes new friends that way. She says she goes to the white church near Pennywell, at Pilton Rise. And the big minister's a hell of a man. Comes from up north. A voice like nothing on earth. Can hear him preaching down at the far end of Pennywell Road! In fact, she says she can hear him from her house!

MOTHER Doesnae have to go to church at all! Och, no. If the church was the only place to meet folk, I'd never get to ken a soul!

NEIGHBOUR They say we'll all end up getting moved out to places like that. Out of here.

MOTHER I'll believe that when it happens.

NEIGHBOUR They've already tried to clear out St Patrick's Square. The University want to take it over. But there's one old guy refusing to budge.

MOTHER Quite right.

NEIGHBOUR It seems he's a cripple, too. Lives on the top flat. But he'd rather drag himself up and down the stairs than move out his house.

MOTHER Must be a stubborn auld customer right enough!

1ST ACTOR (*sings offstage*)
And I will refuse to flit
Heave awa, we're no deid yet!

FATHER No deid yet.

DAUGHTER Overcrowded. Underfed. Sick and tired. But no, we're no deid yet.

(FATHER *enters with friend – neighbour's husband. They go to their wives.*)

FRIEND There's always something makes life worth living. Like beating Hearts in the Scottish Cup! (*puts on green and white scarf*) Come on the Hi-bees!

FATHER (*puts on maroon and white scarf, sings*) Follow! Follow! We will follow Jam Tarts. Everywhere, anywhere, we will follow on!

FRIEND Away you go! We'll murder you in the Cup.

FATHER Rubbish! You havenae got the class. It's only two years since you got relegated.

FRIEND But we got promoted again right away.

FATHER Aye, wi a bit of help from the Hearts.

FRIEND Eh?

FATHER We sold you J J Smith. Best dribbler in the league. (*aside*) But nae finish. Couldnae finish his dinner!

FRIEND He's playing better for us than he ever did for you. Scored a hat-trick against Clyde.

FATHER Well, there you are then! Class! And on top of all that you poached our manager, Willie McCartney.

FRIEND Couldnae get away fae Tynecastle quick enough.

FATHER No, but seriously, you don't really think you've got a chance, do you?

FRIEND We've got Rab Walls and Brick Wallace. They're good for a couple of goals.

FATHER They'll never get it past Jack Harkness.

FRIEND We've got Mickey Langton and Peter Flucker.

FATHER Carthorses the pair of them. Barney Battles'll run rings round them. Bob Johnstone and Willie Murray'll tear them apart.

FRIEND We've got Timothy James O'Keefe. Signed from Waterford.

FATHER Aye because he scored the winning goal against you on your Irish tour. Broke your goalie's finger wi a hard shot.

FRIEND Aye, but the point is, he's playing for us now!

FATHER He kicks wi the left foot of course. (*crosses himself*) Like most of your team.

1ST ACTRESS (*as referee*) Just keep religion out of this, OK?

FATHER OK. We'll do all our talking out on the pitch. Right?

FRIEND Right! (*shouts*) Come on the Hibs!

FATHER Come on the Hearts!

NEIGHBOUR How did the game go?

FRIEND We slaughtered them, nothing each. It was at Easter Road too. Record crowd of 33,000.

FATHER Then in the replay, at Tynecastle, before 41,000, it was Hearts 2 Hibs 0! Johnstone and Murray the scorers. Hullo! We're into the semi finals!

FRIEND Aye, OK.

FATHER Like I said, this team's got class. It's going places.

FRIEND Aye, to Hampden, to get cuffed by Celtic in the semis!

FATHER We're building for the future. We've got this young lad coming through. Tommy Walker he's called. Now this boy is one to watch.

FRIEND I've seen him in the reserves. He's a tumshie. A bit like yourself.

FATHER Now listen you!

FRIEND A puddin.

FATHER You're asking for it!

FRIEND A mug.

FATHER Right! That's it! Outside!

(*They start taking off their jackets, squaring up.*)

MOTHER Will you two behave yourselves! Honest to God! Grown men fighting over a stupid game!

FATHER Nothing stupid about football.

MOTHER No, but if you used half that energy to organise yourselves and fight to change things, we might start getting somewhere!

(DAUGHTERS *march on*)

DAUGHTERS (*sing*)

Vote, vote, vote for Mr Murray!
He is the one we're voting for.
If ye dinnae vote for him,
Then we'll bash your windaes in
And you'll never go to voting any more!

SON It's that time again.

FATHER Elections for the Council.

SON Ach, they're all the same. It's only folk from the moneyed classes that can afford to stand for the Council. Darling and Maul and folk like that.

DAUGHTER Remember Harkess the undertaker!

YOUNGER DAUGHTER Vote for Harkess, He'll bury your Carcass!

DAUGHTER Hugh Harkess, the dead man's friend!

SON He had a sign in his window that said, 'You may pass this way but once, but we'll get you in the end. Join our Christmas Club!'

DAUGHTER What a character, eh?

MOTHER I was reading that Esther Henry's standing as an independent next time.

FATHER Aye, she's what you call a lady of independent means right enough!

MOTHER I heard she just spent six months in South Africa.

FATHER All right for some.

MOTHER Her pal Cormack's standing twice. In Gorgie and North Leith.

SON Can he do that?

MOTHER Nothing to stop him. He's got the money as well. Plenty of rich benefactors.

YOUNGER DAUGHTER Protestant Action are contesting thirteen seats.

DAUGHTER So it could be Protestant Dictator Cormack after all.

FATHER You know, I heard Cormack ranting away at the foot of the Mound last week. And this boy pipes up at the back, says to him, 'Isn't it true that when war comes, a bullet won't discriminate between a Protestant and a Catholic?' And Cormack looks at him, and turns to the crowd, and says, 'I smell a Pape!' And that's all the answer the boy got.

MOTHER Don't talk about war. I don't want to know.

SON The polis are looking sideways at any foreign visitors in case they're spying.

YOUNGER DAUGHTER I spy with my little eye.

SON Merrilees arrested a spy at Waverley station. Dressed himself up as a porter!

YOUNGER DAUGHTER They've even stopped the German oompah bands from playing in the High Street.

DAUGHTER Changed days.

MOTHER I don't want to know.

(*Burst of loud jazz music from radio. They shout lines over it.*)

SON Come on!

FATHER Everything is great!

SON We're no deid yet!

YOUNGER DAUGHTER Live, love, laugh and be happy!

DAUGHTER Changed days!

MOTHER Peace in our time!

(*The radio station is changed and we hear the voice of Prime Minister* NEVILLE CHAMBERLAIN.)

CHAMBERLAIN I am speaking to you from the Cabinet Room of 10 Downing Street. This morning, the British Ambassador in Berlin handed the German government a final note stating that, unless we heard from them by eleven o'clock that they were prepared at once to withdraw their troops from Poland, a state of war would exist between us. I have to tell you now that no such undertaking has been received and that, consequently, this country is at war with Germany.

DAUGHTER History again.

FATHER (*sings*) In 1939 . . .

SON A very good year.

(*sound of siren*)

MOTHER (*covers ears*) Don't!

FATHER In 1939 . . .

DAUGHTER Blackout!

(*Blackout. Siren continues.*)

INTERVAL

# ACT TWO

(*Voice of* RADIO ANNOUNCER *is heard.*)

ANNOUNCER This is the BBC Home Service. We're interrupting programmes to make the following announcement. It is understood that, in accordance with arrangements between the three great powers, an official announcement will be broadcast by the Prime Minister at three o'clock tomorrow, Tuesday afternoon, the eighth of May. In view of this fact, tomorrow, Tuesday, will be treated as Victory in Europe Day.

ALL (*sing*)
Happy days are here again
Skies above are clear again
Our lives are full of cheer again
Happy days are here again.

1ST ACTOR No more blackouts.

2ND ACTRESS No more lying listening out for the bombers.

2ND ACTOR No more rationing.

2ND ACTRESS It'll be changed days right enough.

ALL Changed days!

(*cheers*)

1ST ACTRESS Hey, you should see it down Princes Street. You canny move for folk. Absolutely chocablock.

1ST ACTOR It's the same all over the city. Parties in every street.

1ST ACTRESS Well how about making this one go with a swing! (*to audience*) Come on! Don't sit there with your faces tripping yous. The war is over!

ALL (*sing*)

Roll out the barrel
We'll have a barrel of fun
Roll out the barrel
We'll have the blues on the run.

2ND ACTRESS Hey, d'you know what we did? We knew this was coming, right? So a few of the lassies started saving up. Put by a shilling a week. And we promised ourselves when the war ended we'd go into a pub, cause we'd never been to one before. So that's what we did. We were going to the Labour Halls in Musselburgh, and we stopped off at the Bluebell. Course we didnae know what to order. Hadn't a clue! So we asked these two old ladies, and they said, 'You should try a black and tan.' Well, we had no idea what it was, and most of us just ordered a shandy, or a sherry, or a glass of port. But two of the lassies thought, 'To hell with it!' and they ordered these black and tans. And the man brought them in these big big tumblers! They nearly died! Anyway, by the time we got to the Labour Halls we were all laughing and singing and having a right carry on, and they wouldnae let us in, cause they said we were too drunk. All except the two that had had the black and tans. They just marched right in, nice as you like! And they were drunker than the rest of us!
(*sings*)

Show me the way to go home
I'm tired and I wanna go to bed
I had a little drink about an hour ago
And it's gone right to my head.

Two black and tans please!

(3RD ACTRESS *puts on black shawl, becomes Italian woman.*)

2ND ACTOR Hey, missis! Have ye no heard the war's finished? Are ye no gonnae join in our wee bit celebration?

1ST ACTRESS Shoosh! Don't! That's yon Italian wifie.

ITALIAN WOMAN I'm glad your war is over. I'm glad there is to be no more killing. But don't expect me to dance and sing.

1ST ACTRESS Her man went down on the Arandora Star.

ITALIAN WOMAN They were all rounded up, all the men. Just because of their nationality. They were put in a ship, the Arandora Star. They were being deported to Canada, for internment.

1ST ACTRESS The ship never made it. Was sunk by a German U-boat.

ITALIAN WOMAN They were all chained together in the hold. Drowned like rats.

2ND ACTOR Victory in Europe.

2ND ACTRESS Love and laughter. Peace ever after.

1ST ACTRESS She's no the only one that doesn't feel like celebrating. A hell of a lot of good men didn't come back.

2ND ACTRESS Bravest street in the world.

2ND ACTOR Happy days. Here again.

1ST ACTOR Of course the war's changed everything. Nothing is the same. I mean, you can't go back, can you?

2ND ACTOR I'll tell you one thing though. Cormack and his lot are bombed out. Nobody takes him seriously any more. I mean, can you imagine? He went round telling people they should bayonet the Papes first and then fight off the Germans!

1ST ACTOR Oh he still makes his speeches at the Mound. Rants on about nuns flushing their babies down the toilet! But he's just regarded as a joke.

3RD ACTRESS If folk learned anything from the war it's that they have to pull together, and never mind all this stupid sectarian nonsense.

1ST ACTRESS We're all in the same boat.

2ND ACTRESS All in it together.

2ND ACTOR And no deid yet!

ALL Right!

2ND ACTRESS (*looks about*) The place wasn't flattened by bombs. Glasgow got the worst of that. So the slums were still with us. In fact they were worse than ever.

1ST ACTRESS Six more years of neglect.

1ST ACTOR I came back from the war, in my demob suit, and it was depressing. Back to the same poky wee hole to find it had deteriorated even more.

3RD ACTRESS Scotland's brave highway.

1ST ACTRESS Oh, they've built the West Grantons and the Niddrie Mains and the Prestonfields, but they've hardly even touched the problem.

LABOUR SPOKESMAN We will, my friend. The new Labour government will tackle it head on.

2ND ACTRESS Nye Bevan said it would be sorted out in four or five years. But nobody really had a clue. Folk were living in appalling conditions, and just having to make the best of it. Something drastic had to be done. It was a matter of throwing up as many houses as possible, as quickly as they could.

3RD ACTRESS Never mind the quality!

LABOUR SPOKESMAN Oh, you can sneer. But I'm telling you, even the worst of what was put up was ten thousand percent better than what these folk were moving out of. And anyway, a lot of it was meant to be temporary, buy some breathing space – maybe 20 or 30 years – give us time to work out the next move.

2ND ACTRESS Breathing space! Sounds nice.

3RD ACTRESS Fresh air.

(*change in lighting*)

WOMAN They've offered us a house in Pennywell.

HUSBAND Where's that about?

WOMAN Well, I asked how much it was on the bus and the man said threeha'pence.

HUSBAND Oh well, it costs your sister threepence to Craigmillar, so it canny be as far as that.

WOMAN West Pilton they call it. I think it's one of the most futuristic schemes ever built. That big park in the middle of West Pilton Circus. It's got a bowling green in it, tennis courts, football pitch, running track. Plenty swings and that. And all the houses look onto it. It's lovely.

2ND ACTRESS Breathing space.

WOMAN Aye.

NEIGHBOUR We're out at Drylaw. Got a lovely view right down the Forth. Right out to sea. You can see the ships passing right by. There's one – the Corunna it's called. Beautiful. Looks like a floating palace. You can even hear the dance band music on it. The thing is, they're talking about building more houses right across the road. It'll spoil the view completely. Still. That's progress, eh?

DAUGHTER It's *great* out here, isn't it?

WOMAN Well . . .

DAUGHTER We've got a bath and everything. You're not frightened to get up and go to the toilet in the middle of the night! And the house is that big! It's like a palace! You can run about fae room to room!

WOMAN Aye, making a racket and getting under my feet!

DAUGHTER And if you go out, there's all the building sites where they're putting up the new houses. It's just one big playground!

WOMAN Until the watchie catches you and gives you a thick ear.

NEIGHBOUR Are ye no liking it out here then?

WOMAN Och, it's just, we're an awful long way from the town, you know. You look about you and it's awful bare.

NEIGHBOUR Och, that'll change. The place'll get bigger.

HUSBAND No *too* big I hope.

NEIGHBOUR And they'll provide more amenities – shops and pictures and pubs and everything. Won't have to go all the way into town for a wee bit entertainment.

WOMAN You miss things like that, don't you?

HUSBAND You're no gonnae get all nostalgic about that bug-ridden pit are you!

WOMAN No the house. I wouldnae want to go back to that. It's the atmosphere, and just, *knowing* everybody. Mind the laughs we used to have? The wee sing-songs . . .

DAUGHTER The games of forfeits!

WOMAN Aye! Or even just folk dropping in for a blether. Now what have I got for company? The wireless!

(*Theme music – Housewife's Choice*)

(THREE WOMEN *in identical sets – small formica-top table and kitchen chair in same colour. Their moves are choreographed – they are separate but parallel – as they respond in turn to the announcer's remarks.*)

ANNOUNCER Good morning . . . I feel very important today in being asked to start this new series. The BBC have now decided to do something for the real backbone of the country – the woman who spends her time between getting her children ready for school, cooking her husband's dinner, and standing in a queue to get something to give him that dinner with. In other words – the British Housewife!

WOMAN You don't know the half of it. The amount of stuff that's still on ration! Meat, butter, sugar, you name it. And you canny get an egg for love or money.

ANNOUNCER Every weekday morning we are going to give you 50 minutes of records of your own choosing, at a time when we hope you will be able to listen. Obviously it won't suit all of you, but there's at least a chance that some of you have got rid of your husbands and children, and you can sit down for a little time and listen to the kind of music you have chosen for yourselves.

1ST NEIGHBOUR You're kidding!

ANNOUNCER And I must say that your choices have delighted me! They are so classical and discriminating. Not that the most popular artists like Bing, Spike Jones and the Ink Spots have been left out. But you have gone for more recognised masterpieces.

2ND NEIGHBOUR Oh aye?

ANNOUNCER Anyway, without further talk, I'm going to plunge straight into the first record. It's a nice tune for this time of day . . .

WOMAN Oh God, is that the time already!

ANNOUNCER And what I like about it is that it is essentially English. And when I say English I mean English and not British!

ALL THREE WOMEN Huh!

ANNOUNCER A very old tune called *Greensleeves*, which has been asked for by Mrs Barbour of Regents Park, London NW1, and many other housewives.

(*Tape – 'Greensleeves'*)

WOMAN (*She talks over tape.*) Disnae look like much of a day for drying. (*looks out*) Still, maybe I'll take a chance. No that anybody about here would take it in for me if the rain did come on. And it's no as if I'll be back quick, by the time I queue for this and queue for that. What am I gonnae make for the tea? Suppose it'll depend what I can get. Just a matter of eking it out. Now where was that thing I saw in the paper? A recipe for pancakes wi no eggs and very little fat. (*finds paper*) Here it is . . . 'Warning . . . Do not try this unless you are absolutely desperate.' Recipe for disaster more like!

2ND NEIGHBOUR (*indicates radio*) Would that no make you greet? You'd think they could put on something a wee bit cheerier!

WOMAN And God knows we need a bit cheering up. (*turns dial to change channel*)

NEWSCASTER And in his speech last night, Mr Attlee had a special message for women . . .

2ND NEIGHBOUR What's he on about now?

NEWSCASTER 'I appeal to women . . .

WOMAN Oh does he now?

NEWSCASTER . . . to remain at, or to go back to work during this difficult period. I am not asking anyone to neglect that most important national service, work in the home. But I hope those who can will continue as they did in the war.'

WOMAN Great! As if it's no bad enough without being made to feel guilty! (*switches off*)

1ST NEIGHBOUR (*picks up newspaper and flicks through*) Would you credit it? It says here that in Denmark you can get as many eggs as you like, out of a slot machine! Just put in threepence and there you are. It says meat, eggs and cheese are not rationed, only butter, and even then you get nine ounces a week. Nine ounces!

2ND NEIGHBOUR (*flicks through paper*) Listen to this. Professor such-and-such of Vienna, the inventor of synthetic oil, has invented synthetic meat, made from wood! I think he's already been selling it to our butcher! (*chucks down paper*)

WOMAN Wonder what he's playing now. (*switches on radio*)

(*Tape – Inkspots – 'I'll Get By'*)

Poverty may come to me, it's true
But what care I? Say I'll get by
As long as I have you.

1ST NEIGHBOUR (*She has been listening, dreamy, lost in the music.*) Lovely. (*becomes aware of time*) Here, I better get a move on. I canny sit about all day being 'classical and discriminating'.

ANNOUNCER I think you'll want to listen to the next one.

1ST NEIGHBOUR Will I?

ANNOUNCER It's Bing Crosby and the Andrews Sisters, with a bit of sound advice for all of us in these times.

(*Tape – 'Accentuate the Positive'*)

(*The* THREE WOMEN *go into an Andrews Sisters routine, miming or singing along.*)

(*Tape*)

Accentuate the positive
Eliminate the negative
Latch on to the affirmative
Don't mess with Mr in-between . . .

WOMAN We hear you Bing! We never died a winter yet!

2ND NEIGHBOUR We got by.

1ST NEIGHBOUR We survived.

WOMAN We managed.

1ST NEIGHBOUR We scrimped and scraped.

2ND NEIGHBOUR We made do.

WOMAN We made it into . . .

ALL The Fifties!

(*Tape – Fifties jazz. The* THREE WOMEN *do a quick change into bright coloured skirts.* WOMAN, HUSBAND *and* DAUGHTER *sit looking proudly at 'TV' in corner.*)

WOMAN The first telly in the stair!

HUSBAND The neighbours can come round and watch the Coronation.

DAUGHTER We got the day off school *and* a tin of sweeties wi the Queen on the lid *and* a threepenny bit!

WOMAN There's talk about having a street party.

HUSBAND Just like the old days, eh?

WOMAN Roll out the barrel!

HUSBAND I told you you'd get to like this place.

WOMAN Och, we've got decent folk round about. That's half the battle.

NEIGHBOUR (*entering*) Have you got it working?

HUSBAND I've just got to fix the aerial.

NEIGHBOUR Shouldn't it go outside, on the roof?

HUSBAND You can get an outside aerial, but it's dearer. We should be OK wi this. With it being quite open here, and us being on the top flat, the guy in the shop said we should get a picture no bother. There! (*switches on*) He said it takes a minute or two to warm up. (*They stare at set.*)

2ND ACTOR Five minutes later!

NEIGHBOUR A minute or two?

HUSBAND Aye, well.

DAUGHTER Looks like a snowstorm.

WOMAN Must be snowing in London!

NEIGHBOUR In June!

HUSBAND It should just be a matter of moving the aerial, finding the right position. (*moves about the room with it*)

WOMAN There's something!

HUSBAND What?

WOMAN A sort of a squiggle.

HUSBAND Great! (*tries again*)

NEIGHBOUR Come on! It'll be starting in a minute!

HUSBAND I'm doing my best!

(*He continues trying aerial in different places.*)

WOMAN There! No, you've lost it.

(*By now he is up on a chair, arms at full stretch*)

NEIGHBOUR That's it! If you can just hold it there.

DAUGHTER Look, there's the coach! You can see it!

HUSBAND My arms are gonnae drop off!

WOMAN Hold still and stop jooking about!

NEIGHBOUR There!

WOMAN Stand up. It's the National Anthem. (*They stand and sing – 'God Save the Queen'.*)

(HUSBAND *falls from chair.*)

DAUGHTER Dad!

HUSBAND (*to audience*) Eventually we got an outside aerial. And a bigger set. 12 inch screen!

WOMAN You'll never guess who's on the telly tonight.

DAUGHTER Muffin the Mule!

WOMAN Mrs Connery's boy Tam.

NEIGHBOUR I heard he was an actor right enough.

WOMAN Calls himself Sean these days. That's his stage name.

HUSBAND Nom-de-plume sort of thing. Like what you use for putting on your line at the bookies.

WOMAN Something like that, aye. Here, look, it's in the paper.

HUSBAND (*reads*) 'Requiem for a Heavyweight. Edinburgh-born actor Sean Connery . . .'

WOMAN That's him!

HUSBAND '. . . plays a boxer who must decide whether he will heed his doctor's warning that he must not fight again.' Sounds good.

DAUGHTER (*looks over his shoulder at paper*) It's on after 'What's my Line?'

HUSBAND Aw naw!

WOMAN What is it?

HUSBAND Your old man said he'd be round the night.

WOMAN So what?

HUSBAND I want to see this play.

WOMAN Maybe he'll like it. It's about boxing.

HUSBAND Aye but you know what he's like. He's no very fond of the telly at the best of times. Thinks it's watching him! And you canny get him to shut up when it's on. He blethers away nineteen to the dozen.

NEIGHBOUR Poor auld soul.

HUSBAND Bloody auld nuisance!

(*doorbell off*)

DAUGHTER I'll get it! (*runs off*)

WOMAN (*to husband*) You keep a civil tongue in your heid!

DAUGHTER (*comes back with old man*)
It's Granda.

WOMAN Come in, da, and sit yourself down. Cup of tea?

GRANDA I wouldnae say no.

WOMAN There's a good play on the night. About boxing.

GRANDA On the wireless?

HUSBAND The telly.

GRANDA That thing! I canny be bothered wi it. Load of rubbish that's on it.

WOMAN This has got Mrs Connery's boy in it. Big Tam. Only he's called Sean.

GRANDA Tam Connery? He's no a boxer.

WOMAN No, he's an actor. (*patient*) He's kidding on. It's a play.

GRANDA Couldnae punch his way out a paper bag.

NEIGHBOUR Away ye go! He's a big strong man.

GRANDA Ach, they're all the same these actors. Nancy-boys the lot ae them.

WOMAN Da!

NEIGHBOUR What about John Wayne then?

GRANDA Aye, well he's different. The exception proves the rule, doesn't it?

HUSBAND Rubbish!

GRANDA Aye, that's what this play'll be. A lot of rubbish. I'd rather listen to the wireless. 'Bing Sings' is on the night.

HUSBAND Well we're watching the play and that's final.

(*They are all seated on settee, eyes glued on TV.*)

DAUGHTER Eamonn Andrews is boring.

NEIGHBOUR I think he's nice.

GRANDA Used to be a good boxing commentator before he started this lark.

WOMAN When does the play start?

HUSBAND After this.

DAUGHTER Wish it would hurry up.

WOMAN Have you finished your homework?

DAUGHTER I'll do it later.

WOMAN At ten o'clock?

DAUGHTER I'll do it in the morning then. It's hardly anything.

HUSBAND Well, make sure you do.

WOMAN I was reading that the part of this boxer was supposed to be played by Jack Palance. You know him that's always the baddy in the cowboy pictures.

GRANDA I like a good cowboy picture.

WOMAN Anyway, it seems he couldnae do it. Had to back out at the last minute.

GRANDA Shane . . . Stagecoach . . .

WOMAN And that's how Tam got the part. The director's wife remembered being in a play with him. And that was it. A foot in the door.

HUSBAND A nod's as good as a wink, eh?

GRANDA Gunfight at the OK Corral . . .

HUSBAND Here, it's starting. Shoosh!

(*They watch.*)

GRANDA Bing'll be singing on the wireless.

(*sings*)

Where the blue of the night
meets the gold of the day
someone waits for me . . .

NEIGHBOUR Be quiet!

DAUGHTER Aw what's up wi the picture?

HUSBAND It's her downstairs wi her blooming hoover. I've *told* her it causes interference, but she won't listen. In one ear and out the other! (*He picks up brush, starts banging on floor with handle. All stamp on floor in unison.*)

WOMAN That's better. It's settled down.

DAUGHTER There he is!

NEIGHBOUR Big Tam!

WOMAN And to think he used to deliver our milk!

HUSBAND He's playing 'Mountain McClintock'.

GRANDA He doesnae even look like a boxer.

ALL Shoosh!

GRANDA Is that supposed to be a gym? I don't know! (*The others, rivetted to the screen, ignore him as he continues.*)

I used to go to Charlie Cotter's in Leith Street. That's where I learned to box. Oh aye, I knew them all. Charlie Cotter, Paddy Fee, Tansy Lee, Bertie Mackie – him that writes for the 'Dispatch'. And they didnae half put you through your paces! Started out wi skipping and shadow-boxing, and all these floor exercises, to build up these muscles here, the ones that protect the solar plexus. There's six muscles there. I bet yous didnae know that.

ALL (*rounding on him*) Wheesht!

GRANDA Ach! (*gestures at screen*) That's no real! You know, that thing's the killer o the lot. Kills the imagination. Kills conversation. (*gets up*) I'm away hame, to listen to the wireless.

WOMAN (*Gets up to see him out, but half her attention is still on TV.*) OK da, we'll see you next week.

GRANDA Aye. (*calls back as he leaves*) You get a better picture on the wireless! (*exit*)

WOMAN He's getting addled.

HUSBAND Ach, he's got to stop living in the past. These days are gone, for good. Got to move wi the times. I mean, it's like wanting to stay in the old houses while they disintegrate, fall down about your ears.

NEIGHBOUR Like the Penny Tenement.

HUSBAND The Penny Tenement. It was in the Carnegie Street area. Beaumont Place, off St Leonard's Street. The property was in a terrible state of disrepair. Completely dilapidated. Landlords were legally obliged to keep the buildings wind-and-watertight, fix the drains, that sort of thing.

ROSIE Rosie's the name. Donald Rosie. And yes, I'm the owner of this building. But what the hell am I supposed to do with it? I mean, I can't afford repairs on this scale! So I reads in the paper about this Glasgow M.P. – Willie Reid – that's been ranting on about slum landlords. And I goes to him and I says, 'Right! Here you are. I'll sell you the building for a penny. I'm serious. Give me a penny and it's yours. And *you* can get it repaired! So he shows me the door. Throws me out on my ear. And that's why I've come to you. 'Edinburgh Town Council' I thought. 'They're the boys to deal with it!' I mean it is your responsibility. Or it should be. (*looks about him*) First time I've been in the City Chambers. Very nice it is too. Eh? What's that? Oh aye, sorry. I'm here to make you an offer. Just take the building and it's yours for nothing. Free. Gratis. Buckshee. I don't want a penny for it . . . What? . . . And you!

2ND ACTRESS They showed him the door.

3RD ACTRESS Out on his ear.

1ST ACTRESS So he just skedaddled. Washed his hands of the whole business.

1ST ACTOR And nothing was done about the repairs.

1ST ACTRESS One of the outside walls was shored up in the 1930s, because of a big crack.

2ND ACTRESS And the crack's getting worse. Look at it!

3RD ACTRESS How long do you expect folk to go on living here? I'm telling you, it's downright bloody dangerous!

1ST ACTOR Nothing gets done.

1ST ACTRESS There's water pouring in through the gable.

2ND ACTRESS When you walk you can feel the floor moving under your feet.

3RD ACTRESS The outside wall's bulging away out.

1ST ACTOR Still nothing gets done.

3RD ACTRESS And finally, in the middle of the night . . .

1ST ACTRESS Oh dear God! The building's coming down!

(*Tape – building falling, set collapses, chairs etc. knocked over.*)

1ST ACTOR There was this godalmighty crash, and the whole side of the building collapsed.

3RD ACTRESS The building laid open like a doll's house. As if somebody had taken a knife through it, sliced it in two.

2ND ACTRESS People's belongings hanging out the edge. Cookers, sinks, prams, tin baths.

1ST ACTRESS Folk in their pyjamas, folk stark naked!

1ST ACTOR You can see bedrooms, bits of beds. Would look quite funny if it wasn't so tragic.

3RD ACTRESS The incredible thing is that nobody was killed. Not a soul. Nobody was even that badly hurt. There was just one woman and her baby suffered cuts and bruises. Miraculous really, when you think about it.

2ND ACTOR Nineteen families to be rehoused. Somewhere. Somehow.

2ND ACTRESS Next morning the place is swarming with reporters, photographers, the lot.

1ST ACTRESS This is national news.

2ND ACTOR Of course, in some quarters this kind of publicity was not at all welcome. What with Edinburgh trying to build up its image as the Festival City, the Lord Provost was not too pleased!

1ST ACTRESS But I'd say this was the finest thing that ever happened for Edinburgh's slumdom.

2ND ACTRESS Just a month before this, local councillors had been told it might be twenty years before people in that area could be rehoused. Now the Corporation suddenly had the resources to rehouse hundreds of local families in a matter of months.

3RD ACTRESS Now that's what I call a miracle!

1ST ACTOR This is in 1959.

2ND ACTOR (*sings*) In 1959, it was a very good year . . .

2ND ACTRESS It was the start of the clearance.

3RD ACTRESS Soon there were over 1000 houses demolished, and 2000 people moved out.

HUSBAND (*enters, singing*)

Love is nature's way of giving
A reason to be living
The golden crown
That makes a man a King!

WOMAN I don't need to ask where you've been.

HUSBAND The Doocot. Just nipped in for a quick one.

WOMAN Or two.

HUSBAND That big minister was there. Collecting everybody's rent money out their pay packets. Otherwise they'd spend the lot. He'll be down the Corporation on Monday, paying it for them. That way at least they won't get into arrears.

WOMAN I bet their wives don't see much of what's left in the pay poke.

HUSBAND No, I don't suppose they do. Eh . . . (*fishes in pocket for pay-poke, hands it over*)

WOMAN (*looks inside*) Right.

HUSBAND Place was jampacked the night too.

WOMAN Nowhere else to go, is there?

HUSBAND And there's more and more folk moving out here all the time.

WOMAN What was it they said when we first came? Place'll get bigger. More amenities. Amenities!

HUSBAND Too much too quick. Never learned from anybody else's mistakes. (*exits*)

WOMAN And before you know it, things start going wrong.

(*Enter two other women* – NEIGHBOURS – *one pushing a pram.*)

2ND NEIGHBOUR It's just a general decline in standards. I mean, it used to be you had to keep the place decent. The

Sanitary would be round to check. And woe betide you if your house wasnae up to scratch.

1ST NEIGHBOUR That Sanitary woman used to strike fear into everybody.

2ND NEIGHBOUR Built like a sergeant major she was!

1ST NEIGHBOUR When she stopped coming round, a lot of them didnae bother. Oh, don't get me wrong. The vast majority of folk here are still decent good-living people. But it's just, they used to be more careful about who moved in.

WOMAN You had to prove you could look after the place.

2ND NEIGHBOUR After a while it was just anybody and everybody. And it just takes one bad family to blight a whole stair.

1ST NEIGHBOUR Then the good folk move out and everything goes downhill.

WOMAN At one time the Clerk of Works used to be round here regular, round all the back greens. Told you if he didnae like what he saw. Now when did you last see the Clerk of Works about here?

2ND NEIGHBOUR They don't give a damn anymore. Nobody does. Kids run wild. The place is overrun wi dogs.

1ST NEIGHBOUR I hate that chippy at the Circus. The kids congregate there and then go on the rampage through the scheme. Terrible.

WOMAN See in Edinburgh before the war, most of what you would call teenage crime – young boys and that – happened on a Sunday. It's a fact. The place was dead. Everything was shut. Nothing to do. So they got up to mischief. Well, that's what it's like here. No amenities, nothing. It's like a permanent Sunday! They get bored and they run mad.

1ST NEIGHBOUR And then it starts. A vicious circle. More of the good folk move out, more problem families get dumped here. The heart just goes out of the place. (*crosses stage, pushing pram*)

WOMAN Hope she'll be OK, walking home on her own.

2ND NEIGHBOUR Aye, there's some right nutters about.

WOMAN It's getting that you don't feel safe.

2ND NEIGHBOUR What can you do?

(WOMAN *pushing pram is looking about her, anxiously. Shadowy figure in the background, tailing her.*)

MAN (*approaching her*) Hello there, darling!

(*Pram hood pushed back revealing* MERRILEES *dressed in baby's bonnet.*)

MERRILEES Right! You! (*grabs man by the arm*) Merrilees again. Still on the job. Still a master of the cunning disguise. Still trying to clean up this town and rid it of all undesirable elements – the vermin that infest our streets. (*to man*) So! Consider yourself nicked! There's no escape from the Short Arm of the Law! (*Exit with his prisoner.*)

WOMAN Ach aye. You've got to laugh.

2ND NEIGHBOUR Otherwise you'd greet.

WOMAN Keeping the place decent.

2ND NEIGHBOUR A job and a half.

(COUNCIL WORKMAN *enters, measuring things up, as if for repairs.*)

WORKMAN Of course a lot of this new housing was sub-standard to begin with. Thrown up. Jerry-built.

WOMAN The floors were done wi this mastic asphalt. Supposed to take a month to do it properly. So the boss comes round and says to the workmen, 'Slap it down quick. Do it in a week and I'll make sure you get a good bonus.' So, you see the result. (*indicates*) The floor's anything but smooth. All these wee, like, volcanic eruptions in it. If you laid linoleum on top of it, it would burst through. Then there's the dampness. Condensation.

WORKMAN (*officious*) We advise you not to paper for the first year. Let it dry out.

WOMAN But even after that, it's hopeless. The walls are still wet. And if you do paper, it just peels off.

WORKMAN (*clears throat*) Yes, well, obviously you should just paint the walls. Have you tried stippling? I've heard it's all the rage. You dip a wee sponge in paint and dab it on the wall, make a fancy design. Comes up nice. So I've heard.

WOMAN We've had a meeting about the dampness. We're trying to get the Council to do something about it. They said they'd send a man round, to see for himself.

WORKMAN That's what I'm here for. Now, what seems to be the problem?

WOMAN Well, I've seen me taking my suit out the wardrobe and it's covered wi green mould.

WORKMAN (*noncommittal*) Really?

WOMAN It's a fact.

WORKMAN (*to audience*) You wouldn't believe some of the nonsense these people tell me. I mean, it's obviously their own fault. (*makes notes*)

(*Three separate, parallel interior 'sets', as before.*)

1ST NEIGHBOUR I'm no able to keep food in the kitchen cupboards. They're too damp.

WORKMAN And do you know why that is?

1ST NEIGHBOUR No I don't know why that is. That's what you're here to tell us.

WORKMAN Well, you're supposed to keep the cupboard doors open at all times.

1ST NEIGHBOUR Oh is that right? The kitchen's about eight feet by six, and I'm supposed to leave these four doors open at all times, sticking out to here!

WORKMAN Yes, quite. (*moves on, making notes*)

WOMAN It's the kitchen cupboards.

WORKMAN Ah, yes. I see you've got the doors open. Well, there you are. You're supposed to keep them shut!

WOMAN But . . .

WORKMAN (*he moves on again*) Keep your windows open. (*moves on*) Keep your windows shut. (*moves on*) It's obvious you're making too much soup. (*moves on*) Your kids are taking too many baths.

WOMAN What?

2ND NEIGHBOUR Anything but admit the bloody houses were built wrong in the first place!

WORKMAN I'll be making a full report. You'll be hearing from us. Or not. As the case may be.

(*Tape – 'Telstar', The Tornadoes*)

WOMAN One of the most futuristic schemes ever built, eh? Like living on another planet! Ach aye, it's a tale of two cities right enough. Sometimes I look up towards the town, up at the skyline there, the castle away in the distance, and it's like another world altogether.

2ND ACTOR Edinburgh, the Festival City!

(*Goes into undergraduate revue routine with* 1ST ACTOR *and* 3RD ACTRESS.)

(*sing*)

We've come here for the Festival and Fringe
We've really had a jolly super binge
We're paying through the nose
For a cupboard up a close
And we guarantee our jokes will make you cringe.

2ND ACTOR I say, I say, I say! Why did the cabinet minister cross the road?

1ST ACTOR I don't know. Why did the cabinet minister cross the road?

2ND ACTOR To see the Pristine Peeler!

1ST ACTOR He denies it of course.

3RD ACTRESS Well he would, wouldn't he?

1ST ACTOR Crisis? What crisis?

3RD ACTRESS You've never had it so good!

WOMAN Och, it's getting ridiculous. Next time you go downstairs to use the outside lavvy, you'll find somebody's using it as a Fringe venue!

2ND NEIGHBOUR Och, I like having them about, all the young folk and the tourists and everybody. Makes the place come to life a bit.

WOMAN You know, I've seen some real celebrities here at Festival time. One year I saw Edward G Robinson. Just passed right by there, and I says, 'Hello.' And he smiles and says, 'Hello!' Awful nice he looked. Lovely skin. And another time I saw Robert Mitchum. And I saw Elsie Tanner too. She was lovely. Glamorous, you know.

2ND NEIGHBOUR It definitely does a lot for the city. Brings money into the coffers.

3RD ACTRESS But we've got to think bigger. Do things on a grand scale. What we need is, an Opera House!

2ND ACTRESS (*to audience*) Do you remember the Poole's Synod Hall, at Castle Terrace? That's where we told you to go for tickets to the Masque of Edinburgh in 1929. Just checking, to make sure you've been paying attention out there! Anyway, by the 1960s it was functioning as a cinema.

WOMAN My wee lassie used to sneak in to see the horror films.

1ST ACTOR In 1963, just about the same time the Traverse Theatre opened . . .

WOMAN *That* place?

1ST ACTOR In James's Court.

2ND NEIGHBOUR Where Kelly's Paradise used to be.

WOMAN Say no more.

2ND NEIGHBOUR You can imagine the kind of 'shows' they'll be doing.

WOMAN Ach well, it'll never last.

1ST ACTOR (*butting in*) . . . Just about the same time the Traverse opened . . . they decided they were going to knock down Poole's and build . . .

THREE 'PERFORMERS' A hole in the ground.

(*They sing, to tune of Bernard Cribbins' 'Hole in the Ground'.*)

Well there it was
Bloody great hole
Hole in the ground
Don't ask how many pound
It cost to put it there
It's sort of square
It's the ugliest gap-sight
You'll find anywhere

And along comes this bloke fae the Cooncil
Wi a file that says 'Some of these days'
And he looks down the hole
Poor demented soul
And he says

I can see it all now
Don't ask me how
But I promise you this
It'll be a wow
We've accepted a bid
It's as good as did
And all it's going to cost
Is a million quid.

WOMAN A million quid?

1ST ACTOR And then some.

2ND ACTOR And that's just for starters.

3RD ACTRESS Meanwhile, out in those areas of multiple deprivation!

WOMAN I'd fight anybody that says a word against this place! It's not the place, it's what you make of it. You've got to fight to do something with it, to keep it right! We can have our own Festival out here. We've already got the Gala Day.

FRIEND Out wi the bunting, the banners, the Union Jacks!

WOMAN My wee lassie's been elected Queen! She gets to wear a crown and robes and ride on the float wi her ladies-in-waiting, and everything!

FRIEND Queen for a day. Must be nice.

WOMAN Come on, you always enjoy yourself anyway, wi all the bands and the dancing.

FRIEND And the games.

WOMAN Just like Barrie's trips! Remember them?

FRIEND Do I no just?

(*they sing*)

We're no going to Barrie's Trips
We're no going again . . .

FRIEND Things don't change much, do they?

WOMAN It's good to see the kids enjoying themselves.

FRIEND It's kind of sad all the same.

WOMAN How d'you mean?

FRIEND Och, come Monday morning, all the good clothes go back to the pawn. And it's all over for another year. Back to the grind.

WOMAN Auld claes and porridge!

FRIEND Aye. Och I think the place is starting to get me down. I just wish we could get out, make a fresh start. Go somewhere new.

WOMAN Breathing space.

FRIEND Aye.

(*Planning Committee have seated themselves at table.*)

CHAIRWOMAN Ladies and gentlemen, what we're envisaging here is a new kind of suburb.

1ST OFFICIAL Flats between 2 and 5 storeys, nothing higher, so as not to spoil the magnificent views.

2ND OFFICIAL A park at the southern end of the scheme, and running right up from there, a big wide walkway, 200 feet wide, over a mile long, with open vistas to the Castle, to Craiglockhart, to the Pentlands.

CHAIRWOMAN A Twentieth Century Royal Mile!

1ST OFFICIAL Another road from east to west, with shopping centre, churches, community centre, car park.

2ND OFFICIAL There'll be a corner shop for every 300 houses, built in to the blocks of flats.

CHAIRWOMAN The flats themselves will be modern, easy to heat and look after.

1ST OFFICIAL Allowing for a high level of employment . . .

2ND OFFICIAL . . . and an increase in the number of car owners.

1ST OFFICIAL . . . there will be an average of more than one parking space per house.

CHAIRWOMAN There will be three new primary schools, each with its own nursery.

2ND OFFICIAL Plenty of grassy playing areas for children.

1ST OFFICIAL Squares planted with trees.

2ND OFFICIAL Lots of benches for people just to sit and take the air.

1ST OFFICIAL All in all, a truly desirable place where anybody would be proud to live!

CHAIRWOMAN Ladies and gentlemen, we give you . . .

ALL Wester Hailes!

*(fanfare)*

WOMAN Didn't quite work out the way it was planned, did it?

FRIEND Not exactly.

WOMAN Things never do, do they?

CHAIRWOMAN You can't blame us for everything.

1ST OFFICIAL For instance, there's these new government regulations, about the amount of light coming into a house.

2ND OFFICIAL 'Into a living room in November!'

1ST OFFICIAL So the flats can only face in certain directions.

2ND OFFICIAL And in order to get the same number of houses in . . .

WOMAN You built them higher.

1ST OFFICIAL Exactly!

FRIEND Oh, and that bit about the houses being easy to heat.

CHAIRWOMAN No?

FRIEND Afraid not. In fact they're bloody expensive places to keep warm. And of course there's the perennial problem of the dampness.

WOMAN You tell us to scrub the walls wi bleach to get rid of the black marks. But what do you do when they come back, and keep coming back? Spend all yer time scrubbin the walls?

1ST OFFICIAL You'll just have to keep your windows open.

2ND OFFICIAL Keep your windows shut.

1ST OFFICIAL Cupboards open.

2ND OFFICIAL Cupboards shut.

1ST OFFICIAL Too many baths.

2ND OFFICIAL Too much soup.

FRIEND Same old nonsense.

WOMAN Again.

FRIEND Those corner shops never materialised.

CHAIRWOMAN Weren't allowed within a certain radius of the projected shopping centre.

WOMAN The new Royal Mile never quite made it.

CHAIRWOMAN A lot of trees were planted.

WOMAN But most of them died off.

FRIEND Nobody was appointed to look after them, you see.

CHAIRWOMAN Quite.

FRIEND There's the odd patch of grass, but most of it ends up covered wi rubbish, broken bottles.

WOMAN 'A truly desirable place.'

FRIEND Golden City.

(FOOTBALL SUPPORTERS *enter, scarves round wrists.*)

HIBS SUPPORTER
Seven-nil, seven-nil, seven-nil!
Seven-nil, seven-nil, seven-nil!

(*Laughs at Hearts supporter*)

HEARTS SUPPORTER Awright! You caught us on an off day.

HIBS SUPPORTER Oh aye! We scored seven lucky goals!

HEARTS SUPPORTER Christ!

HIBS SUPPORTER Ea-sy! Ea-sy!

(HEARTS SUPPORTER *exits*)

HIBS SUPPORTER Canny take it, eh! (*to audience*) At Tynecastle too! What a way to start the year! (*sings*) Westering home on a 33 bus . . . (*exit*)

WOMAN You quite finished? (*shakes head*) You get folk that don't even like to admit they live in Wester Hailes. They'll say they live in the Calders, or Sighthill.

FRIEND Our first house was in the Calders. It was that roomy. You could all sit down at the same time in the same room!

WOMAN Up here's skimpier somehow, especially the high flats.

FRIEND The thing is, I was glad to get a house out here. It's nice and open and light.

CHAIRWOMAN There we are!

FRIEND And the way it's all laid out in wee squares. You don't have to worry about the kids playing in front of cars, or wandering about. You see them playing and you know they're safe.

CHAIRWOMAN Exactly the way we planned it!

WOMAN It's different in the high flats. Westburn and that.

CHAIRWOMAN Oh.

WOMAN Got to drill them at the door before they go out. 'Don't go round any corners! Stay right down there where I can see you!' Because it's all the same! Once you go round a corner you don't know if it's your block or somebody else's block. I mean I get lost!

VISITOR (*entering*) Excuse me. Where's Hailesland Place?

FRIEND Up there. Second on your left.

VISITOR Thanks. (*exit*)

MAN I was on the squad that built they high flats. I bet if you bang your walls you'll hear them rattling, wi all the beer cans we left in there! We'd sit and drink our cans and chuck the empties in between the walls!

FRIEND Cavity wall insulation right enough!

MAN I worked on the building of the shopping centre as well.

FRIEND I wouldnae go telling folk that!

CHAIRWOMAN Originally we had a different plan for the centre. But the designer . . . eh . . . died on us.

WOMAN Explains a lot!

MAN It was about the last thing to be built too.

WOMAN Typical.

FRIEND In fact they built the pub before they built the shopping centre!

WOMAN Enough said!

FRIEND Mind before the centre opened, you had to use the one down at Sighthill. On a Friday night you'd see a big convoy of empty prams going down there!

WOMAN And full ones coming back! I used to take glucose tablets to do the shopping! I'm no kidding! I'd go down to

Sighthill and get loaded up wi messages. And coming back up that hill, it was really, really steep. I was like this! So I got doped up on dextrosol!

FRIEND Dextrosol was it?

MAN As long as that's all you were taking!

WOMAN Doped up.

FRIEND Some folk were.

MAN To the eyeballs.

WOMAN They started calling this place Vallium City.

FRIEND Mother's Little Helper.

WOMAN Housewife's Choice!

FRIEND The harling's off the walls. The ceiling's letting in. The kitchen's rotten wi damp.

MAN Just keep taking the tablets.

WOMAN 25 percent unemployment.

FRIEND Kids growing up. No prospects. No future.

WOMAN Nothing.

*(Tape – Sex Pistols – 'Pretty Vacant'. Music comes down a little, for voice over.)*

GLUESNIFFER I was sniffing glue when I was still at primary school. Just for a laugh, you know. Something to do. All your mates are doing it, so you give it a try. Then you just move on fae there. Try other things. Guys come round the schools and that. Pushing. Only this stuff costs money. And if you're no working, you've got to get the money somewhere else. So you start nicking things. Then you break into a house or two. And most of your money's going to this dealer, and you think, Maybe I should start dealing myself. So you get some and you go round the schools. And it goes on like that.

FRIEND Vicious circle.

WOMAN Vicious.

*(Music up again, louder. Then fade.)*

CHAIRWOMAN I think the scale of the problem's exaggerated. It's no worse here than anywhere else. It's just that you've got the best part of 20,000 people concentrated in quite a small area.

VISITOR *(entering)* Excuse me, how do I get to Hailesland Place?

CHAIRWOMAN Down there. Second on your right.

VISITOR Thanks. *(exit)*

CHAIRWOMAN Where was I?

FRIEND Scale of the problem.

WOMAN Exaggerated.

CHAIRWOMAN Yes.

MAN 25 percent unemployment. More if you count the folk that are on temporary schemes.

FRIEND To keep the figures down.

WOMAN Job creation.

CHAIRWOMAN That's what we need! Get the people without jobs to work on brightening the place up! All these boulders that the builders dug up. We can have them placed in the middle of the squares.

FRIEND They're all right. Gives the weans something else to play on. Climbing up. Playing at mountaineers.

MAN Bloody eyesore if you ask me. Should do something about them.

WOMAN Make the place look drabber than ever.

CHAIRWOMAN We can paint them! *(exit)*

WOMAN In the name of God!

FRIEND Painted them all these hideous bright colours.

MAN Like Noddy's toytown.

FRIEND Never asked us.

WOMAN Just thought it was a good idea.

MAN Planners rule, OK.

FRIEND Aye, well. The planners made this place the mess it was to begin with.

MAN And made a lot of money out of it!

WOMAN But a lot of us have moved here from places wi a strong sense of community.

MAN Like the Old Town.

WOMAN And we've brought that with us, OK? And it's people that make a community. And we're gonnae adapt to what we've got and build this place up. And we'll do it ourselves!

MAN We're no deid yet!

FRIEND We got ourselves organised.

WOMAN Tenants associations.

MAN A newspaper. The Sentinel.

WOMAN The school was a big help.

FRIEND WHEC.

MAN A community school.

FRIEND Wi a cafe, a library, a swimming pool.

WOMAN For everybody.

MAN Except the first time I went there, to set up a summer playschool, this janny that looks like Fred Flintstone grabs me by the lapels and says 'What are you doing messing up my school?' *His* school!

VISITOR (*entering*) Where's Hailesland Place about?

WOMAN Don't know. Sorry.

(*exit* VISITOR)

(SCHOOLGIRL *enters, blows rasping note on saxophone, attempts scale.*)

WOMAN What a racket!

SCHOOLGIRL If I keep practising I'll be as good as Tommy Smith.

FRIEND Who's Tommy Smith when he's at home?

SCHOOLGIRL Boy in my class at school. He's brilliant.

WOMAN Oh aye?

SCHOOLGIRL No, but I mean *really* brilliant. The teacher said when he was fourteen that was it. There was no more she could teach him, he was that good.

MAN Is that right?

SCHOOLGIRL Now's there's talk of him going to some music school in America. If they can raise the money to send him.

FRIEND If who can raise it?

SCHOOLGIRL The folk in Wester Hailes. Everybody.

WOMAN The Sentinel ran a campaign. And the money started coming in. They had whip-rounds in the pubs, in shops, in the school.

MAN And they did it. They raised enough. Three thousand quid!

WOMAN The boy was on his way.

FRIEND Is he really that good?

MAN You think he canny be because he comes from here?

FRIEND Well . . .

SCHOOLGIRL He's in America now. Berkeley. And some of the top musicians in the world are saying he's one of the best. I'm telling you, this boy is gonnae make it to the big time. There's no limit. New York, London, Tokyo. You never know, he might even be accepted in Edinburgh!

(*Tape – Tommy Smith – 'Forward Motion' album*)

VISITOR Listen. Where's Hailesland Place?

SCHOOLGIRL Up there, over the flyover . . .

WOMAN Down the steps . . .

MAN Across the square, through the underpass . . .

FRIEND Then double back, and disappear up your own . . .

VISITOR Forget it! How do I get out of here?

SCHOOLGIRL You could take up the saxophone!

(*music continues*)

2ND ACTRESS I think it's time to take a daunner back into the Old Town. See what's been happening there.

1ST ACTRESS We can get a number 30 from just outside the shopping centre.

2ND ACTRESS 40 pence

1ST ACTRESS Takes us right back into the High Street.

2ND ACTRESS We're into the 1980s now, aren't we?

1ST ACTRESS That's right.

2ND ACTRESS Up to date.

1ST ACTRESS More or less.

2ND ACTRESS There's been some changes about here anyway. Look at all these banners.

(*Song – reggae/calypso beat*)

(1ST & 2ND ACTORS, 3RD ACTRESS *sing*)

There's a red flag flying in the Royal Mile
Above the City Chambers, that should make you smile!
The Tories have labelled us 'a bunch of yobs'
But we're Improving Services Creating Jobs!

(*They strike various social-realist-poster kind of poses – clenched fist etc.*)

3RD ACTRESS Supporting the Arts!

1ST ACTOR Supporting Sport!

3RD ACTRESS It's your equal-opportunities . . .

2ND ACTOR . . . whatever-your-class-creed-colour-gender-or-sexual-orientation . . .

1ST ACTOR . . . anti-apartheid . . .

3RD ACTRESS . . . nuclear-free . . .

2ND ACTOR . . . creative accounting . . .

3RD ACTRESS . . . local authority!

FRIEND Vandals, that's what I'd call them. Defacing all our beautiful buildings with their banners and propaganda. Make the place look like some East European satellite state.

WOMAN Away you go. It's the best thing that ever happened to this place. A good shake-up. Breath of fresh air.

FRIEND (*reads slogan*) Count me in?

WOMAN More slogans. Who the hell's Ed Burgh?

FRIEND Did somebody get paid for dreaming that one up?

WOMAN A Glaswegian.

FRIEND It figures!

COUNCILLOR There's been a lot of development about here.

FRIEND Aye. It's quite a fashionable place to live now.

COUNCILLOR (*moves chairs into position for meeting of reminiscence group*) If you'd like to take a seat. I'm sure the others won't be long.

WOMAN Och, they'd be late for their own funerals!

COUNCILLOR What I'd like to talk about is the changes you've seen.

FRIEND Changes!

WOMAN I was talking to this lassie the other day, and she says to me, completely deadpan like, 'Oh, I've just moved in to this lovely wee executive flat in St Mary's Street, quite delightful so it is.' St Mary's Street!

FRIEND Suppose it'll be all bistros and wine bars next.

WOMAN Soon be as bad as Glasgow!

FRIEND Or Leith!

WOMAN Och, you wouldnae ken the place.

FRIEND I suppose it's nice enough, but . . .

(*Other* OLD FOLK *enter, exchange greetings, sit down.*)

COUNCILLOR The Council's trying to avoid the London Docklands situation here. Trying to keep the right social mix. I mean, some of you are still in the same houses that you've lived in all your days.

FRIEND But it's not the same.

WOMAN No heart.

OLD WOMAN Used to be a real community you know. Full of life. Full of character.

FRIEND Teeming.

OLD MAN Not now.

FRIEND There's no shops for one thing. Well, not real shops.

WOMAN It's all antiques and tartan gift shops and places selling fancy knitwear.

OLD MAN There's the odd Paki shop of course. Couldn't do without them. But when you remember the place, the way it used to be. Butchers and Bakers and Candlestick Makers. The lot!

OLD WOMAN Campbell's the Butchers.

WOMAN And Wilson's.

OLD MAN And Davie's.

FRIEND McAdam's the Bakers.

OLD WOMAN And Cameron's.

COUNCILLOR Candlestick Makers?

OLD WOMAN Well, maybe no! But there was just about everything else.

OLD MAN Hendry's the Grocers.

FRIEND McAndrew's.

OLD MAN The two Miss Burns's newspaper shop.

WOMAN Tony's the ice-cream shop.

OLD MAN Donati the chip shop.

FRIEND Vipen the wee sweetie shop. Used to get macaroon there. If you got one that was pink inside, you got another one free. I remember that!

OLD WOMAN Then there was Granny Meikle's.

FRIEND All the sweeties in jars.

OLD MAN Magic.

WOMAN No wonder shops was something we played at.

OLD WOMAN Down the canal basin at Tollcross. That place was a wonderland! In amongst all the rubble you'd get lovely coloured stones. And you'd take another stone and champ it down into powder. Golden maybe. Or brick red. Really lovely. And you'd lay it all out in wee jars that you got from your mother. And you'd put like granite chips in another jar. And your pals would say, 'I'll have half a pound of that.' And you'd have a wee spoon to measure it out into a poke made out of newspaper. And you'd use bits of broken crockery for money. A bit wi a gold rim on it would be a pound.

OLD MAN Times were hard, but somehow life was simpler.

COUNCILLOR Of course the summers were longer then.

OLD WOMAN Of course!

FRIEND And warmer.

OLD WOMAN Much!

COUNCILLOR Ach aye, nostalgia's not what it used to be!

WOMAN Naw!

COUNCILLOR Well, thanks for your memories!

OLD MAN Not at all son, thank *you*.

(*They shift chairs, move off.*)

1ST ACTRESS Listen.

1ST ACTOR What?

1ST ACTRESS We've been doing a bit of jooking about in time here.

1ST ACTOR Aye.

1ST ACTRESS Well I was wondering . . .

1ST ACTOR Uh huh?

1ST ACTRESS Any chance of having a wee look at the future? Just a few years down the road I mean. See where it's all going,

1ST ACTOR Why not? Ladies and Gentlemen . . . The Future!

(*Presentation* – 1ST & 2ND ACTORS, 2ND ACTRESS *are carrying lavish PR folders.*)

1ST ACTOR Welcome to the Royal Mile Theme Park!

2ND ACTRESS After restoration and gentrification, we bring you Disneyfication!

2ND ACTOR Six hundred and sixty six years of Edinburgh's history, from the granting of the City's Charter by Robert the Bruce . . .

1ST ACTOR See our historical pageant! See history in the making!

3RD ACTRESS Is this no where we came in?

1ST ACTOR Come with us down the Royal Mile of memory . . .

1ST ACTRESS This is definitely where we came in. (*exit*)

1ST ACTOR See the living tableau unfold, as actors portray Saint Margaret, Malcolm Canmore, Robert the Bruce . . .

2ND ACTRESS Knox and Mary . . .

2ND ACTOR Burns and Scott . . .

2ND ACTRESS Gardyloo!

1ST ACTOR Visit a re-creation of Stevenson's Treasure Island in the Nor Loch. We decided to re-flood it a couple a years back. It had such potential!

2ND ACTRESS Come on our 'Bodysnatchers' night-time tour of the city. Rob graves with Burke and Hare!

2ND ACTOR Visit the city's only hospital, with its huge maternity unit – the Malcolm Rifkind Memorial Ward.

1ST ACTOR Fly from the Niddry Street Heliport to your luxury hotel accommodation overlooking the Firth of Forth . . .

2ND ACTOR The Pilton Hilton . . .

2ND ACTRESS And from there to our Outreach Centres . . .

2ND ACTOR Leith Marina and the Wester Hailes Safari Park.

2ND ACTRESS And back down the Royal Mile, where one of the most charming features is *Old Town Folk*, a hologrammatic re-creation of life from the 1920s on.

2ND ACTOR Feel the teeming life.

1ST ACTOR See the characters.

2ND ACTRESS A typical family in their typical Room and Kitchen.

2ND ACTOR With our special feature, Bowfaround, smell the stovies, the sheep's heid broth.

2ND ACTRESS All this and more, for your education and delight.

1ST ACTOR And today, I am happy to announce that we have with us a very special guest. (*hushed reverent tones*) Ladies and gentlemen, the last remaining indigenous resident of the Old Town. (*ushers her to seat*) (*aside*) They couldn't get her to move out. Kept muttering about being 'no deid yet.' (*to* WOMAN) Now, we're very honoured to have you here with us. And I just want to ask one question. What was it like?

(*Spot on* WOMAN, *close in on her face as she speaks. Others step into background, speak as ghostly voices from the dark.*)

WOMAN It wasnae all happy days right enough. About eighteen children, maybe nine of us survived. The place was hotching. The rats had a swimming gala!

2ND ACTOR Folk were sociable. Looked out for one another.

2ND ACTRESS Always a big pot of soup on the go.

1ST ACTOR Hunger's good kitchen.

3RD ACTRESS Like an Irishman's parlour.

1ST ACTOR Scotch or Irish? Wallop!

2ND ACTRESS Fresh buckies.

1ST ACTOR Skeechan shandy.

WOMAN A pennyworth of soor dook.

1ST ACTOR Burn-the-bible. Choke-the-chicken.

WOMAN Hop-step-and-birl!

2ND ACTOR You don't know things are difficult. What's difficult? Everything is great!

2ND ACTRESS (*sings*)

The wind, the wind, the wind blows high.
The snow comes falling from the sky.

3RD ACTRESS The R101 flew overhead. The size of it, drifting past.

2ND ACTOR Down in flames.

1ST ACTOR We heard it on the crystal set. The cat's whiskers!

WOMAN Thought we were rich. The pennies smelled of gas.

2ND ACTRESS A shilling fry out the butcher's.

1ST ACTOR Do not pawn these boots!

WOMAN Barrie's Trips, wi my tinny on a bit of tape.

2ND ACTRESS (*sings*) We're no awa tae bide awa!

WOMAN It always comes on rain!

2ND ACTRESS Girl of the Golden City.

3RD ACTRESS The Blessed Margaret Sinclair, died at 25.

1ST ACTOR No Popery!

2ND ACTRESS And the hungry marchers.

2ND ACTOR Swept under the carpet.

3RD ACTRESS Polishing the brasses and blacking the range.

WOMAN Out to the dancing.

2ND ACTOR Fairlies.

3RD ACTRESS The Marine.

2ND ACTRESS The pictures twice in a blue moon.

3RD ACTRESS Tom Mix at the Starry.

2ND ACTOR Saturday night sing-songs.

2ND ACTRESS (*sings*)

When I grow too old to dream
I'll have you to remember.

1ST ACTOR Games of forfeits. Games of cards.

WOMAN Was never the same after the War.

2ND ACTRESS Two black and tans!

WOMAN Lot of good men never came back.

2ND ACTOR And it all changed. Folk moving out.

1ST ACTOR Refuse to flit!

2ND ACTRESS But it was breathing space.

3RD ACTRESS A lovely view, right out to sea.

WOMAN They all moved out.

2ND ACTRESS We made do.

3RD ACTRESS We survived.

WOMAN And we had the Festival. All the young folk and the tourists. I saw Robert Mitchum once. And Elsie Tanner. I've seen them all come and go. And I'm still here.

ALL (*quietly*) No deid yet!

WOMAN And there's nowhere I'd rather live. (*pause*)

Can I tell you a story?
A Glasgow man and an Edinburgh man die and go to Heaven.
And St Peter says to the Glasgow man, 'Where d'you come from?'

And he says, 'Glasgow'.
And St Peter says, 'Fine. Come in.'
And he says to Edinburgh man, 'And where do you come from?'
And the man says, 'Edinburgh.'
And St Peter says, 'Fine. You can come in. But you'll no like it!'
It wouldnae compare, you see.

(*Sings, and others join in.*)

If ae decreed that I should walk
But just one mile each day
And I with age and sorrow weighed
Forgive my choice of way
I'd choose from every mile I've crossed
On land or sea or air
The mile that makes a Scotsman proud
Of Edinburgh fair
O let me walk the Royal Mile
That's Scotland's brave highway
Where at one o'clock from the Castle rock
Comes Auld Reekie's call each day
And as the echo sounds
In the Palace grounds
Then the heavens on Scotland smile
And you've made your day
In the royal way
On the Royal Mile
Yes you've made your day
In the royal way
On the Royal Mile.

(*Cut lights abruptly to black on last word of song.*)

END